ECONOMIC EDUCATION

 T5-AFS-530

Exam : June

Table of contents

Cooperative for the Development of Instructional Materials

PRODUCTION

This workbook version of **ECONOMIC EDUCATION** has been developed by Brian Maddock.

It represents a complete revision of the original textbook which was developed by the following teachers and consultants and published in three booklets in 1983.

Rafeek Ali	Lindsay Place High School
John Allen	Laval Catholic High School
Rocco Barbieri	Montreal Catholic School Commission
Pasquale Bavota	Verdun Catholic High School
Terry Brennan	Loyola High School
Michael Carley	Baldwin-Cartier School Commission
Dave Chandler	Rosemere High School
Murray Clark	John Rennie High School
Susan Cloghesy	St. Pius X Comprehensive High School
George Cripps	Richelieu Valley Regional High School
David Dyson	Jérôme LeRoyer School Commission
Jill Guedon	Herzliah High School
Grant Hawley	Chateauguay Valley Regional High School
Ron Hellstrom	Riverdale High School
Steve Macknish	Bishop's College School
Brian Maddock	Lakeshore School Board
Wendell McDougall	Pierrefonds Comprehensive High School
Lloyd McGuire	LaSalle Catholic High School
Lou McGuire	Macdonald-Cartier High School
Dennis Mullen	Beaconsfield High School
Donna Pasteris	William Hingston Comprehensive High School
Margaret Peyton	Hudson High School
Suzanne Roth	Protestant School Board of Greater Montreal
Jan Sobanski	Lester B. Pearson High School
Leslie Steventon	Lindsay Place High School
Will VanBiljouw	Father McDonald Comprehensive High School
Anthony Wignall	Sir Winston Churchill High School
Lawrence Wood	John Rennie High School

Our thanks go to Geoffrey Rose of Riverdale High School for his advice and practical suggestions for the 1998 revision.

Up-dated 1994
Up-dated and reset 1998
Up-dated 2000
Up-dated and reset 2004

© Cooperative for the Development of Instructional Materials

Distributed by Brian Maddock
141 York
Beaconsfield, QC
H9W 4L3

ISBN 0-921731-18-3

Dépôt légal: 3e trimestre, 1987
Bibliothèque nationale du Québec
National Library of Canada

Module 1

ECONOMIC

ORGANIZATION

OBJECTIVES

1.1   *Explain the bases of economic organization.*

1.2   *Describe and explain the main characteristics of socio-economic organization.*

This first module introduces you to the basic elements of the economy. It explains the main concepts and shows how they are interrelated. Later modules will examine these concepts in greater detail.

You will first discover why an economic system is necessary before comparing different types of economic systems. The roles played by different forms of business organizations and the role of money in our economy will be described. Finally a method of measuring the importance of an economy will be investigated.

Human needs and wants

OUTLINE

Needs
- **Basic needs** are essential for survival. If we were very poor or stranded on a deserted island we would find we could manage without many of the things we presently enjoy, but there are three *basic needs* that we all must have to survive. They are **food, shelter**, and **clothing**.

- *Basic needs* are not identical for everyone; we say that they are **relative**. Our clothing needs are different in summer and in winter. A farm worker needs more food than an office employee. The shelter provided by our homes in Québec with its long, cold winters is different from the shelter provided by a house in the tropics. Nevertheless, it remains true that all people have the same *basic needs*: namely, food, shelter, and clothing.

Wants
- People also desire things which are less essential. We call this desire for things our **wants**.
  Most people have many *wants* such as:
    > a good lifestyle
    > worthwhile leisure activities
    > a job
    > good self-esteem
    > security and a group of friends
    > material possessions such as a car, smart clothes, labour-saving gadgets
    > videos, sports equipment, cosmetics

- *Wants* are desirable, but not essential for survival. We could manage without them.

- *Wants* are also **relative**. Each individual has wants that are different. These differences depend on our age, sex, income, personal preferences, and the type of group we are part of.

- *Wants* are **unlimited**. Each of us has many wants, things we desire to have. When we satisfy one of our wants, another takes its place. There is no limit to the extent of our desires. If you receive a new suit for your birthday then you may want new shoes, or a new handbag, or a new windbreaker, or a different colour of nail polish.

- The more we are able to satisfy our unlimited wants the higher is **our standard of living**. In a developed nation with a diversified economy people are able to satisfy more of their wants than people can in a less-developed country with a lower standard of living.

Individual needs and collective needs
- Each person has **individual needs and wants**: e.g. cosmetics, preferred types of food, medical care, a specific type of car, a certain book.

- As a group or a society we have **collective needs** such as roads, hospitals, parks, libraries, public transportation.

TERMS

Explain these terms in your own words:

basic needs _____

wants _____

standard of living

_____

APPLICATION

1. Compare the relative basic needs of a person living in southern Québec and a person living in a tropical rainforest area in central Africa.

BASIC NEEDS	SOUTHERN QUÉBEC	CENTRAL AFRICA
Food	water, 4 food groups	water, 4 food groups
Shelter	insulated houses for the long winter	walls and a floor to protect from animals & weather
Clothing	shirt, pants, jacket for winter, footwear	shirt, pants, footwear

2. Give examples of:
   a) your individual wants at the present time

   1 _nice clothes_ 2 _cosmetics_ 3 _yoga classes_ 4 _dance classes_ 5 _sports equipment_

   b) collective needs of the community where you live

   1 _roads_ 2 _hospital_ 3 _library_ 4 _park_ 5 _public transportation_

3. To illustrate that wants are unlimited, assume you have been given one of the following as a present:
   - an expensive camera
   - a VCR
   - cross-country skis

   List some other things you will now want to be able to make good use of your present.

   1 _jacket_ 4 _goggles_

   2 _snow pants_ 5 _ski pass_

   3 _helmet_ 6 _gloves_

4. To show that wants are relative, decide which item in the list would likely be most wanted by each of the persons described below.
   LIST: a doll, cosmetics, a set of golf clubs, a hearing aid, a bicycle

   a) a 3 year old girl _a doll_

   b) a 12 year old boy _a bicycle_

   c) a young woman _cosmetics_

   d) a 35 year old man _a set of golf clubs_

   e) a man aged 75 _a hearing aid_

Goods, services, resources, scarcity, and choice

OUTLINE

Goods and services

- To satisfy our needs and wants we buy goods and **services**. The **resources** of the economy are used to produce these goods and services. Because the resources are **scarce** we cannot fulfil all our basic needs and unlimited wants, so as consumers we are forced to make a **choice**.

- **Goods** are concrete and tangible; they have body or substance. Some goods last a long time and are replaced only after a long period; these are referred to as **durable goods**. Others are used up immediately or wear out quickly. These are called **non-durable goods** or *consumables* or *perishables*.

- **Services** are activities which are helpful or useful to others.

Resources

- Society uses its resources to produce the goods and services needed to fulfil our needs and wants. Usually resources are divided into three types:

- **Natural resources** include land and anything that is found in or on the land in a natural state.
  - Anything that exists without being produced by human labour is a *natural resource*.
  - These gifts of nature include forests, mineral deposits, and the power of waterfalls and rivers.

- **Human resources** is a term referring to the population. Only a part of the total population is productive *(involved in producing goods and services)*. This productive sector is often called **labour** instead of *human resources*.
  - The quality of the labour force depends to an important degree on its level of education and training.
  - Examples of *human resources* are: miner, secretary, driver, nurse, carpenter, accountant.

- **Capital resources** involve those things needed by labour to manufacture the goods and services which are then purchased. They are also called **capital goods** or **capital equipment** because they are the tools and machinery needed to produce a good or service.
  - Examples of *capital resources* are: oven, forge, generator, metro-car, computer, truck. It also includes the roads, airports, electricity transmission lines, railway cars, telephone cables, etc. that facilitate the production of goods and services.

Factors of production

- *Human resources, capital resources*, and *natural resources* are together referred to as the **factors of production**.

- To coordinate these three resources in the process of manufacturing goods and services is the function of **management**. Examples of *managers* include foremen, company presidents, store managers, school principals.

Scarcity

- Because our wants are continually expanding, they are inevitably greater than the existing resources. This creates the phenomenon of **scarcity** which is the basis of our economic system. There are not enough goods and services to satisfy all the needs and wants of all the consumers. If there were no *scarcity*, there would be no economic system.

- The measure of the scarcity of a good or service is its *economic value* or **price**. The taste of filet mignon is preferred by some people to that of hamburger. However, there is a greater quantity of steer meat available for the production of hamburger than for filet mignon. Scarcity results in a higher *economic value* for an equal portion of filet mignon and a lower *economic value* or *price* for an equal portion of hamburger.

- Those goods which are found in abundance in nature are referred to as **free goods**. Because these goods are found in unlimited quantities in nature they have no economic value. There are few examples left in industrialized countries, but air is an example.

- Those goods which have some degree of scarcity and therefore an economic value can be referred to as **economic goods**.

Choice
- The basic economic problem results from the interaction of the forces introduced above. People's wants are unlimited while goods and services are scarce or limited.

- As a consequence, people must make a **choice** of which goods they will acquire because of their limited ability to pay for them.

- In other words, the consumer has to make a *sacrifice* or **trade-off**. To acquire the goods and services he wants most of all with the limited funds available, he has to give up, at least for the time being, his less essential wants. Economists call this the **opportunity cost**. Every time you decide to satisfy one want rather than another you are giving up the opportunity to have something else you wanted. Its *opportunity cost* is the item or items that you chose to do without in order to get it.

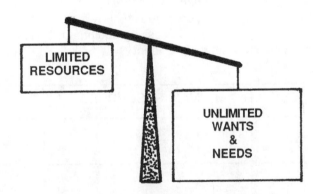

The economic problem: SCARCITY

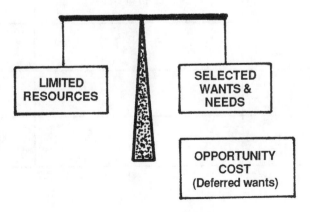

The solution: CHOICE

APPLICATION

1. Match the following examples with the correct terms:

   Examples: money   television   ~~teaching~~   sunshine   photocopier   salesman

   Terms: Human resource   *salesman*   Capital resource   *photocopier/money*

            Durable good   *television*   Service   *teaching*

            Free good   *sunshine*

2. Decide whether each of the following is a **good** or a **service**. Write the letters G or S to indicate your choice.

ITEM	G / S	ITEM	G / S
candy	G	coke drink	G
repair of a car engine	S	toothpaste	G
dental checkup	S	delivery of a parcel	S
advertisement in a newspaper	S	school desk	G
plane trip	S	telephone	G

3. Classify the following items into the three categories in the table below.

   ~~trees~~   ~~cement mixer~~   ~~electrician~~
   lawyer   ~~iron ore deposit~~   ~~factory building~~
   ~~office cleaner~~   ~~word processing equipment~~   long-distance bus
   water in the Manicouagan River   ~~bank president~~   ~~sand on a public beach~~

NATURAL RESOURCES	HUMAN RESOURCES	CAPITAL RESOURCES
trees	lawyer	word processing equip
water in Man.	office cleaner	factory building
sand	electrician	long-d. bus
iron ore dep.	bank president	cement mixer

8

4. **Capital goods** are used to produce goods and services over a period of time.
   Consumer goods are bought by consumers for their individual use.

   Decide whether each item listed below is a capital good or a consumer good.
   Write *capital* or *consumer* next to each item.

   a) high-speed train _____Cap._____ b) taxi _____cap_____

   c) family car _____Con_____ d) TV set at home _____Con_____

   e) TV set in a hotel room _____cap._____ f) your dad's suit _____Con_____

   g) doorman's uniform _____Cap._____ h) farmer's tractor _____Cap_____

   i) your lawn mower _____Con_____ j) office computer _____Cap_____

   k) video game in an arcade _____Cap_____ l) pool table at home _____Con_____

   m) factory building _____Cap_____ n) house _____Con_____

   o) golf ball _____Con._____ p) golf course _____Cap_____

5. You have just won $1000. You have a list of some things you would like to have and you have also found out the prices.

LIST	
New clothes	$120
Canoe	$400
Ski equipment	$250
Video cassette recorder	$950
Computer	$800
Computer printer	$350
Trip to Toronto	$280
Save to buy Christmas presents	$200

   770
   970

   a) What will you choose to buy?

   _____new threads, canoe, ski equipment, christmas presents_____

   b) What is the opportunity cost of your choice? (List the items.)

   _____video cassette recorde, compute, computer printer, trip to Toronto_____

6. Tim and Mary invited some friends for a barbecue. They bought hamburger meat, onions, tomatoes, and buns from the supermarket. They collected dead branches and logs to make a fire. They borrowed a mixing bowl, plates, and cooking utensils from Tim's mother. Mary's father gave them $10 to buy the food. They would have liked to buy three cases of drinks but there was only enough money to purchase one.

   Identify in this story an example of:

   a) natural resource _____logs_____ b) human resource _____Tim + Mary_____

   c) capital good _____barbecue_____ d) free good _____fire_____

   e) management _____Tim + Mary_____ f) scarcity _____money_____

   g) choice _____drinks_____ h) opportunity cost _____drinks (2 cases)_____

7. Use the labels listed below to complete the diagram which illustrates the relationships between wants, needs, resources, scarcity, and choice.

Labels to be inserted in the appropriate box on the diagram:

CAPITAL RESOURCES   LIMITED   SCARCITY

CHOICE   NATURAL RESOURCES   UNLIMITED

LABOUR   NEEDS   WANTS

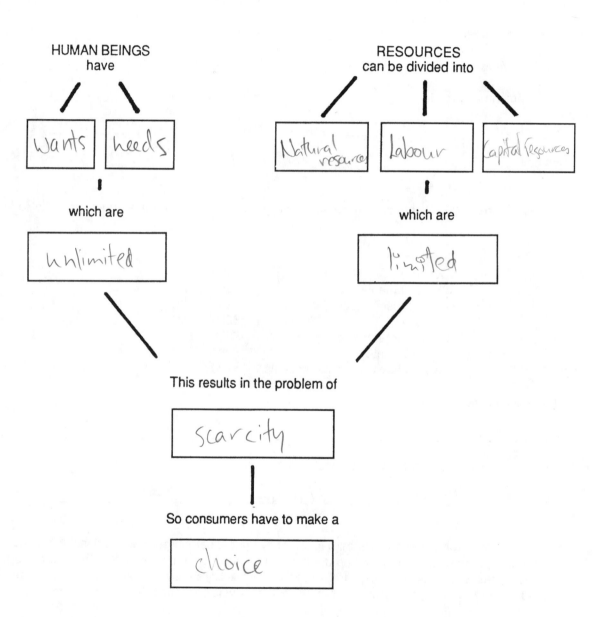

HUMAN BEINGS
have

| wants | needs |

which are

| unlimited |

RESOURCES
can be divided into

| Natural resources | Labour | Capital resources |

which are

| limited |

This results in the problem of

| scarcity |

So consumers have to make a

| choice |

Determination of price: - supply and demand

OUTLINE

Prices! Prices! The consumer complains that the prices of wanted goods and services are too high. The store owner complains that if he has to sell his goods at lower prices he will be out of business. If this is the case, how are prices determined?

Prices are determined in the **market** *(any place where buyers and sellers come together to exchange goods and services)*. The **price** *(what the seller asks the purchaser to pay)* is determined by the **demand** for the good or service and by the **supply** available at a given time. The price changes as demand or supply conditions vary.

The law of supply and demand
- The **demand** is the quantity of a good or service that customers are willing and able to purchase at a given time. The demand is different as the price of the good changes. If plotted on a graph, this produces a **demand curve**.

  • As the price gets lower demand increases

  • As the price gets higher demand decreases.

THE DEMAND CURVE

- The **supply** is the quantity of a good or service that is offered for sale at a given time. The supply is also affected by changes in price. This relationship is illustrated on a graph by the **supply curve**.

  • As the price rises the supply tends to increase.

  • As the price drops the supply tends to decrease.

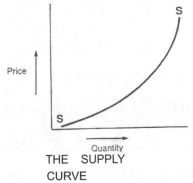

THE   SUPPLY
CURVE

- If we combine the two graphs, the demand curve and the supply curve intersect. The point where they meet is called the **equilibrium point**. The *equilibrium point* indicates the **price** at which the buyer and the seller agree to make an exchange. We sometimes say that the market is then at rest - buyers and sellers have agreed on a price.

  • As the price falls demand increases
  • As the price rises demand falls.
  • As prices rise the supply increases.
  • As prices fall the supply decreases

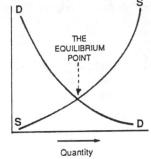

THE
EQUILIBRIUM
POINT

11

- Any changes in supply and/or demand will affect this equilibrium. This is the **law of supply and demand**:

> THE LAW OF SUPPLY AND DEMAND
> - If demand increases prices tend to rise.
> - If demand decreases prices tend to fall.
> - If supply increases prices tend to fall.
> - If supply decreases prices tend to rise.

TERMS

Use your own words to explain the relationship between:

supply and **demand** _____

_____

_____

price and the
equilibrium point _____

_____

_____

APPLICATION

1. Forecast what will happen to the <u>demand</u>:

   a) for sports cars if the price drops by 20% _____

   b) for gasoline if the price rises 100% in the space of six months _____

2. Forecast what will happen to the <u>supply</u>:

   a) of luxury cars if most people refuse to pay over $40 000 for one _____

   b) of waterbeds if people are willing to pay more than the current price _____

3. Forecast what will happen to the <u>price</u>:

   a) of fashion clothes if three new dress stores open in the same mall _____

   b) of video cassette recorders if imports from Japan are restricted _____

   c) of cola-type soft drinks if too many people switch to drinking fruit juices _____

4. A large manufacturer produced 100 000 pairs of blue jeans in readiness for the next season. Unfortunately blue jeans went out of fashion. Even at a reduced price of $25 a pair it was difficult to move the inventory. How does the law of supply and demand explain this situation?

   _____

5. A famous designer produced 500 pairs of exclusive blue jeans with his well-known logo prominently displayed on them. He soon sold all the jeans for $200 a pair. How does the law of supply and demand explain this situation?

   _____

Determination of price: - types of markets

OUTLINE

In our society, there are many types of markets. **Markets** are characterized by the number of sellers and buyers, and also by accessibility. The type of market plays an important role in the setting of price.

Pure competition

- The most desirable market is one known as a purely competitive market or free market. **Pure competition** exists when there are many sellers and many buyers. In this type of market, individual consumers and sellers have no influence on the price of goods and services. The price has already been set by all the buyers and sellers. The set price is accepted by all individuals.
- If a store owner raises his price, the consumers will go elsewhere to purchase the products they need.
- If the price of the product is set too low, the sellers reduce the supply of that particular product to avoid losing money.
- Although there are no true examples of this type of market, one that comes close is the market for fruits and vegetables.

Monopolistic competition

- More usually there are many small businesses who supply similar goods and services (competition). Entry of new businesses is easy (competition). However businesses can differentiate themselves from competitors by a preferred location, by a distinctive quality of their product, or by good service. Consumers often have a personal preference for one supplier (monopoly).
- Prices are kept within a small range by the competition. As long as its prices are not too high a business can retain a monopoly of trade with its faithful customers despite the existence of many competitors. Examples are fast-food outlets, hairdressers, clothing stores.

Monopoly

- A **monopoly** exists when there is only one supplier in the market. *Monopoly* is the opposite of a purely competitive market.
- Examples: *Hydro-Québec* is the sole supplier of electricity in the province of Québec. *Bell Canada* is the only supplier of local telephone service available to subscribers in much of Québec.
- In theory, these monopolies could set much higher prices and get them because there is no alternative supplier, but in practice they are controlled to a degree by government bodies and by consumers' willingness to go without them if the rates are too high.

Oligopoly

- An *oligopoly* is a small powerful group. The type of market that has only a few sellers and many buyers is called an **oligopoly**.
- Examples: the big automobile manufacturers of North America, the two large brewing companies in Canada, the big oil companies which supply gasoline and other oil products. The sugar refiners and the tobacco manufacturers are other examples of oligopolies.
- In an oligopoly it is easy for the few suppliers to agree on prices, how much to offer for sale, and what the quality shall be. At times they may even agree to divide up the market and to reduce competition. This type of **collusion** is considered an unfair business practice and is illegal.

Other factors which help determine prices

- The market and the law of supply and demand are not the only factors that determine prices. Other important factors are:
- **Governments** frequently intervene to prevent free competition among companies. They regulate telephone rates, rents, the price of certain products. This is usually done with the support of the consumers and against the protestations of the businesses involved and also of people who believe in free enterprise.
- **Cartels** are organizations set up to control prices. The oil-producing countries set up an organization called OPEC *(Organization of Petroleum Exporting Countries)* to maintain the price of crude oil at the highest possible level. Cartels can sometimes maintain unreasonably high prices.
- **Unions** and management sometimes enter into contracts which affect the prices of products.
- **Abnormal situations** such as a late frost, a drought, a plant disease, a fire, a war can greatly reduce the supply of a commodity and make it very scarce.
- **Changes in fashion** or the **introduction of new technology** can cause some goods to lose value.

TERMS

Use your own words to explain the difference between a **monopoly** and a **purely competitive market**.

_____

_____

_____

APPLICATION

1. Think of some of the companies and businesses in your area and try to classify them into the three categories of the table below. Think of businesses that provide services as well as those who produce consumer goods.

MONOPOLIES (no competition)	OLIGOPOLIES (few competitors)	FREE MARKET (many competitors)

2. With which type of market would you associate each of the following enterprises?
   Write _monopoly, oligopoly_, or _free competition_ on the line provided beside each example.

   a) The local outlet of the _Société des alcools du Québec_ _____

   b) Your local convenience store _(dépanneur)_ _____

   c) The Montréal Expos baseball team _____

   d) Your barber or hairdresser _____

   e) The gasoline stations in your community _____

   f) The fast-food restaurants in your community _____

   g) The funeral director(s) in your community _____

   h) The radio stations in your community _____

3. Use arrows to indicate your predictions of what will happen to demand, supply, and price of the items named in each of the following situations.

↑ = tend to increase   ↓ = tend to decrease   → = little change

	DEMAND	SUPPLY	PRICE
a) SKIS in a winter with little snow			
b) SWIMSUITS in a hot, sunny summer			
c) APPLES when frost has destroyed 50% of the crop			
d) BAGGY PANTS once they are no longer in fashion			
e) TICKETS to a one-performance only concert by a very popular international rock band			
f) CIGARETTES soon after the government has increased the tax by 50 cents a package			
g) CHRISTMAS CARDS in early January			
h) HAMBURGERS at McDonald's restaurant when Harvey's open a new branch across the street			
i) HOUSES when many families decide to sell and leave the community			
j) SECOND-HAND JAPANESE CARS if the government puts a quota (limit) on the number of new cars which can be imported each year			
k) SMALL CARS when gasoline prices increase sharply			
l) SOFT DRINKS when all workers in the industry get a 20% wage increase			
m) GASOLINE if the supplies from the producing areas are cut off as a result of a local war			
n) HOLIDAYS IN EUROPE if the value of the Canadian dollar is low in relation to the value of the pound sterling and the euro			

Economic factors

OUTLINE

Certain groups play an important part in determining how the economy operates. Sometimes these groups are called **economic factors** or **economic agents**. The principal *economic factors* or *agents* are business firms, consumers, workers, and governments.

Business firms

- They use capital resources, materials, and human resources to **supply** the goods and services within our economic system.
- They are owned and operated by **entrepreneurs** or people who are willing to take risks in producing goods or providing services in return for possible **profits**.

Consumers

- They represent the **demand** side in the exchange of the goods and services produced. It is chiefly the consumers who determine:
    - what goods and services should be produced and in what quantities
    - what the market price should be for the goods and services
    - what quality and styles they would like
- Changes in the buying habits of consumers can lead to great increases or decreases in demand. These changes may create problems such as bankruptcy, inflation, unemployment, and even recession.

Workers

- They provide the **labour** which is essential for the production of the goods and services in the economic system. Workers supply the knowledge and skills as well as the physical labour required.
- All workers in any phase of production - whether they be typists, machine operators, storeroom clerks, or truck drivers - are productively employed because they help to **produce** the articles coming from the company's plant.
- For their contribution they are rewarded with wages, salaries, usually with pensions when they retire, and sometimes with bonuses and shares in the company.
- These rewards are used to buy goods and services, to pay taxes to governments, and sometimes to invest in shares and the ownership of businesses.

Governments

- They operate at various levels *(federal, provincial, municipal)* and play an important role in the economy. Their primary motive is more to **regulate** the economy than to make a profit.
- Governments are engaged in the production of goods and services side by side with private enterprise. They provide services such as operating a system of schools and hospitals, constructing and maintaining roads, building and operating penitentiaries and parks, providing police and garbage collection services. They own and operate some businesses as **crown corporations**.
- Governments collect **taxes** and **duties** of many kinds from consumers *(sales taxes, licence fees)*, workers *(income taxes)*, and companies *(business and corporate taxes)*. They use this money to provide many services. They also use it to pay pensions, employment insurance, and welfare payments for those in need. Grants and special funds are made available to individuals and companies to promote economic growth.
- Governments try to distribute economic wealth more equitably.

APPLICATION

1. All the economic factors are interrelated. There are many links between the various agents in our economic system. Give examples of links or interrelationships that exist between:

    a) businesses and consumers

    _____

    _____

    b) businesses and workers

    _____

    _____

    c) businesses and governments

    _____

    _____

    d) consumers and governments

    _____

    _____

    e) workers and governments

    _____

    _____

    f) consumers and workers

    _____

    _____

2. Choose a product (such as a car) **and** a service (such as a haircut) that you know well. Decide how each of the four principal economic factors applies in each case you choose.

Type of product	FACTOR	Type of service . . . .
	BUSINESS	
	CONSUMERS	
	WORKERS	
	GOVERNMENT	

Economic organization and the division of labour

OUTLINE

Each society has to face a basic economic problem: how to produce and distribute the goods and services needed or wanted by the people. Each society develops an **economic organization** or way of using its economic resources to produce the required goods and services.

The *economic organization* is not the same in all societies, and throughout the history of a given society the system of economic organization evolves *(changes gradually)* over a period of time.

Economic organization in a traditional society

- This system was very common throughout most of history. It has largely disappeared but is still found to some extent in countries where the economy is based mainly on agriculture.
- It is based on subsistence; people try to be as **self-sufficient** as possible. They produce nearly all the goods and services they need with little or no help from outside. Most workers are able to perform many different tasks.
- Most people have to spend much of their time working to produce the goods required to meet their basic needs. All except the youngest children have to work. There is little time for leisure activities.
- A few **artisans** produce specialized products e.g. pottery, metal goods, cloth, leather goods. They perform all steps in the production process, usually with fairly simple tools. They require many hours to produce only a few products.
- When goods or services are exchanged, **barter** *(trading one product for another without the use of money as a medium of exchange)* is often involved.
- The standard of living of most people is not high.

Economic organization in an industrialized society

- In modern industrialized societies most production processes are **mechanized** and workers tend to be specialized. A worker performs only part of the total job, but he does his task very quickly and very efficiently. Economists call this specialization in a small part of the production process "division of labour".
- **Division of labour** has several <u>advantages</u>:
  - It increases productivity because workers become very skilled.
  - It produces a large quantity of standardized products all of the same quality.
  - It reduces labour costs.
  - It tends to lower the cost of goods and thus raises the standard of living.
  - It is easier to train workers to perform one small specialized operation.
  - It keeps all of the machinery busy most of the time so it makes good use of capital resources.
- **Division of labour** also has <u>disadvantages</u>:
  - It often results in boring repetitious tasks, especially for workers on a **production line** which goes along at the same relentless speed all the time.
  - It is necessary for each worker to keep pace with others who are dependent on his output. Quality may suffer in order to produce goods more quickly.
  - It results in less pride in one's work because each worker plays only a very small part in making the final product.
  - It is necessary to find markets for the large quantity of products mass-produced by the factory.

- The number of working hours has gradually been reduced to an average between 30 and 45 hours a week depending on the occupation. Most young people under 18 years old are receiving a full-time education. There is a fair amount of leisure time for most workers.

- The standard of living is reasonably high for most people.

- **Money** is the medium used to help people exchange the specialized goods and services they produce.

Economic organization in a society with high technology

- Some believe we have now moved into another phase where modern advances in high technology are changing economic organization considerably.
- **Robots** control more and more of the production process. Production is becoming increasingly automated. Fewer production workers are required. **Word processors** and **computers** perform many of the office and administrative tasks formerly done by human beings.
- Fewer workers are needed for production and administration. Increasingly, most jobs will be in the service sector. There should be more leisure time for all.
- We are moving towards an almost **cashless society**. Most financial transactions will involve the electronic transfer of funds using debit cards, credit cards, smart cards, telephone for banking and other transactions, as well as the internet.

APPLICATION

1. Give examples of jobs or companies that:

   a) are organized in a traditional way

   i _____

   ii _____

   b) involve much division of labour and extensive use of machines

   i _____

   ii _____

   iii _____

   iv _____

   c) use much high technology

   i _____

   ii _____

   iii _____

   iv _____

2. Write sentences to explain the relationship among the three following concepts:

   DIVISION OF LABOUR — SPECIALIZATION — PRODUCTIVITY

   _____

   _____

   _____

   _____

   _____

   _____

The importance of money

OUTLINE

Money is something which is readily acceptable in exchange for goods and services. We usually think of coins and paper money *(banknotes)* issued by the government's central bank, but cheques, credit cards, debit cards, and smart cards fulfil a similar function.

The barter system
- **Barter** is the exchange of goods and services without the use of money.
- The problem of bartering is to find someone who is willing to exchange the good or service you want in return for the good or service you have to offer. The system can be very inconvenient.
- In recent years organizations have been set up to make it simpler for those wishing to barter their surplus goods or services to find others offering products which they want.

A medium of exchange
- A **medium of exchange** is required to overcome the inconveniences posed by bartering. In our society it is *money*. You exchange your product for money, and then you can exchange the money for another product which you want.
- The medium of exchange must be **universally acceptable** *(acceptable to all people in the society)*. It is usually money but in the past it has been seashells, gold nuggets, playing cards, and beaver pelts in certain societies.
- *Money* is preferred as a medium of exchange because:
  - It is easily transportable *(carried around)*.
  - It is easily recognizable but fairly hard to counterfeit.
  - It is relatively scarce because only the federal government is authorized to mint coins and print bills.
  - It is fairly durable (especially coins; bills tend to wear out and have to be replaced).
- Without an accepted medium of exchange, specialization and the division of labour would pose many problems. Industrialized society could not operate without the convenience and functions that money provides.

The functions of money
- *Money* facilitates economic activities in three important ways. It functions as:
  - **a means of exchange** *(spend / earn)*
    - People pay you for your work, your produce, or your services with money. You use money to purchase goods and services for yourself.
  - **a standard of value** *(compare)*
    - Prices are expressed in monetary units. We can quickly compare the values of different products. All products offered for sale have a price or statement of their current value.
  - **a store of value** *(retain)*
    - We may not wish to exchange all our money immediately after receiving it. Normally people are paid or receive their allowance at weekly, biweekly *(every two weeks)*, or monthly intervals. However, they like to spread out purchases over the period of time between paydays.
    - Over a short period money retains its value so we can store purchasing power in the form of money. In the long run, this may not be true because **inflation** *(a sharp increase in the general level of prices)* reduces the value of money.

APPLICATION

1. Think of the ways in which you use money during the course of one day. List examples of:

    a) using money as a medium of exchange

    i _____

    ii _____

    iii _____

    iv _____

    b) as a standard of value

    i _____

    ii _____

    iii _____

    iv _____

    c) as a store of value

    i _____

    ii _____

    iii _____

    iv _____

2. Suppose there was no money available in society. List six ways in which your daily activities would be affected.

    i _____

    ii _____

    iii _____

    iv _____

    v _____

    vi _____

3. Explain why coins made from precious metals became the medium of exchange for most societies.

    _____

    _____

    _____

    _____

The Gross Domestic Product

OUTLINE

How important is our economy? Is it growing? Does it compare favourably with the economies of other countries? How can we measure the size and growth of our economy?

The Gross Domestic Product (GDP)

- Two commonly used indicators of the size and growth of the economic activity in a country are its **gross national product** (GNP) and its **gross domestic product** (GDP). Since 1986, Statistics Canada has used only the GDP because the economic activity of each province is measured in terms of GDP. Most international comparisons use GDP rather then GNP.

- The **GDP** is the total value of all the final goods and services produced **in the country** over the period of one year. To avoid double counting only the values of final products and services are included: e.g. the value of all the computers produced, but not the values of the separate parts such as silicon chips, video display terminals, and keyboards used to construct the computers.

- The **GNP** is the total value of all goods and services produced by the citizens of a country **both inside and outside the country** over a period of one year.

- Government statisticians add up:
    - **the value of purchases by consumers**
        - the price tags of all the goods and services bought by individuals over the course of the year
            + *plus* +
    - **the value of investment expenditures**
        - the cost of capital equipment used to produce goods and services
            + *plus* +
    - **the value of government spending**
        - the cost of the goods and services used or provided by governments
            + *plus* +
    - **the value of exports**
        - the goods and services we sell to other countries bring in money
            - *minus* -
    - **the value of imports**
        - the goods and services we buy from other countries have to be paid for so they are a debit item

The final figure is the *gross domestic product* for that year. It can be compared with figures for previous years and with the GDPs of other countries.

Limitations of the GDP

- The GDP is not a perfect measure of the importance of the economy. Attempting to add up the value of everything produced in an industrialized society is almost impossible.
- Some things not included in the GDP are:
    - the value of all goods and services produced at home by homemakers, do-it-yourselfers, babysitters, etc. (Housework was worth $318.7 billion in 1992 if people had been paid the same rates they earned for work outside the home. A 1994 Statistics Canada report estimated it would cost up to $26 310 a year to pay someone to perform the household duties of a mother with at least one pre-school child.)
    - the value of all goods and services exchanged by bartering
    - the value of all goods and services paid for "under the table" - the so-called **underground economy** which has been growing steadily over the past decade or two. (A 1994 StatsCan report estimates the value of the underground economy at no more than 5% of GDP. The Minister of Revenue estimated the underground economy to be worth over $60 billion a year, or 9% of the GDP.)
    - the value of all goods and services handled illegally by organized crime, drug dealers, and small criminals
    - changes in the value of stocks and bonds
    - personal savings which are not invested

- If we do not allow for growth in the population, changes in the GDP can again prove misleading. Thus, it is also useful to calculate the **GDP per capita**. This is the GDP divided by the country's population; therefore the value of what the Canadian economy produced for every person within the country is shown. This allows us to make comparisons with the GDP per capita of other countries. *(See tables on page 178.)*

- If the value of the GDP is expressed in current dollars the effects of **inflation** *(a general increase in prices)* are not taken into account. If prices have risen sharply over the year, there may not have been much real growth although the monetary value of the GDP has increased considerably. Thus, the real GDP is calculated in terms of **constant dollars** to take inflation into account. Currently, we calculate each year's GDP in terms of 1997 dollars so that we can compare economic growth from year to year much more easily. If we allow for inflation, we can compare our productivity over a period of time.

- The GDP indicates the amount of goods and services produced by a country but it does not indicate anything about the **standard of living** *(the living conditions of a consumer or a nation)* or the **quality of life**. Not all people are part of the work force nor do all receive the same income.

APPLICATION

1. Find the latest figures to complete the table.

Year	2000	2002	Latest
GDP for Canada (current dollars)	1 075 566 m	1 154 949 m	
GDP for Canada (constant 1997 dollars)	1 020 786 m	1 074 516 m	
Canadian GDP per capita (Canadian dollars)	$34 800	$36 600	

2. Refer to Table 1 on page 178 showing data about the GDP for Canada in the last decades.

   a) Does the latest GDP figure indicate real growth? _____

   b) Compared to other periods in the last decades, is present growth reasonable or slow?

   _____

3.   Refer to Table 2 on page 178 showing the GDP per capita for selected countries.

   a) Name at least 6 countries with a GDP per capita that is high like ours.

   _____

   _____

   _____

   b) Name at least 6 countries with a GDP per capita that is much lower than ours.

   _____

   _____

   _____

The chart below attempts to indicate the relationships among the main components in our economic system. Use the following labels to complete the chart.

Labels | BUSINESSES | LIMITED | RESOURCES
| CHOICES | MARKETS | SCARCITY
| CONSUMERS | MONEY | SUPPLY
| DEMAND | NEEDS & WANTS | UNLIMITED
| GOVERNMENTS | PRICES | WORKERS

Human beings have _____

which are _____

human, natural, & capital _____
which are _____

result in the basic
economic problem of _____

which forces consumers
to make _____

They purchase the goods &
services they have chosen
on the _____

PRODUCTION
of goods and services
is influenced by four main
ECONOMIC FACTORS:

are determined by the _____
& _____

CONSUMPTION
of goods and services
is done by _____

_____ is the medium of exchange
which facilitates the system

ORGANIZATION

OF

PRODUCTION

OBJECTIVES

2.1   *Establish the relationship between business and production.*

2.2   *Compare different forms of business organizations in terms of ownership.*

2.3   *Show the importance of business organizations, regardless of size.*

The production of goods and services is essential if human needs are to be satisfied. Many and varied businesses are set up to produce these goods and services. First, this module will show you how a business is set up, how it is operated, and how its level of success can be measured. You will discover how businesses can be owned, organized, and operated in various ways. The importance of the size of businesses will be discussed. Finally, the integration of some of the very large companies will be examined.

Setting up a business

OUTLINE

Production is an economic activity designed to provide the goods or services needed to satisfy some human want. It is a process which involves combining the required resources to manufacture goods or provide services. This process of combining resources to produce needed goods and services is organized by a **business**.

Entrepreneurs

Businesses are set up and operated by people called **entrepreneurs**. Some entrepreneurs see the need for a new type of product and they set up a new business to bring it into production. Others see new possibilities for an existing business so they take it over and announce it is "under new management".

- An entrepreneur is a **risk-taker**; an individual who is willing to risk a possible loss in setting up a line of business because he/she believes that the factors of production can be organized to produce a profit.
- An entrepreneur seeks **profit**. Some like the challenge of organizing labour, natural resources, and capital into a smoothly operating combination, but, in the long run, the survival of the business depends on making a profit.
- An entrepreneur is a **leader**. He/she has the imagination to see the possibilities of the product and is able to work with others to organize its production. He/she is not afraid to make decisions and take initiatives.
- An entrepreneur is **competitive**. Each wants to make the best-selling products and to gain a major share in the market for them.
- Most entrepreneurs are honest and responsible.

Market research

In order to succeed a business must sell its products in sufficient quantities. It cannot operate without customers. To find customers and keep them it conducts **market research**.

- Surveys conducted by telephone or door-to-door interviews provide valuable information about customer preferences.
- Specialized marketing firms can be hired to conduct more detailed surveys.
- Government statistics reveal important trends such as decline in younger age-groups and increase in the number of retired people.
- Determines how many competitors there are likely to be.
- Tries to estimate how many will be able to afford to buy the product at a given price, which age-group is most likely to want the product, what are the prospects for continuing sales.

As a result of market research the entrepreneur decides whether or not to risk entering a new line of business.

Factors of production

Having decided to make a new product the entrepreneur then has to decide how to combine the factors of production. He/she has to make decisions about:

- **Capital resources** (Financial resources)
  - Money is needed to buy **capital goods** *(machines, tools, trucks, etc. to be used in the production process)* and to provide **operating capital** *(to buy materials, pay workers, etc.).*
  - The necessary capital may come entirely from the entrepreneur's savings, but usually some money has to be borrowed from banks or other lending institutions. He/she establishes a **line of credit**. Some entrepreneurs **issue shares** to raise capital for their new enterprise.

- **Labour** (Human resources)
  - Are there enough suitable workers available?
  - Do they possess the necessary skills or will they have to be trained?
  - Are they unionized? How much will they have to be paid?
  - Where will they live if the production site is far from settled areas?

- **Materials** (Natural resources)
  - What materials are needed to make the new product? Where can they be obtained?
  - Does the local area provide some of the needed raw materials?
  - Is there a suitable source of energy? Which source of energy will be the cheapest?
  - Is there a satisfactory transportation system?

Having examined the marketing studies and considered the various factors of production, the entrepreneur must make a decision: - to abandon the project or to proceed? A risk-taker, he/she is constantly on the lookout for an opportunity to turn ideas into profits.

TERMS

Explain these terms in your own words:

entrepreneur _____

business _____

market research _____

APPLICATION

1. List four new products that have reached the market in recent months. What needs are they intended to satisfy? At which age-group are they aimed?

PRODUCT	NEED	AGE GROUP

2. Think of one new product which you believe could be marketed successfully. Design a survey to test its marketability. Who will be surveyed? How? Include at least three questions that you want answered.

_____

_____

_____

_____

_____

27

3. Carla Gucci has designed a new type of mobile home. Through using a very light-weight plastic she has been able to reduce the cost of producing a mobile home by about $10 000. Carla has very little money and no business experience. Shy and retiring, she finds it difficult to work with other people until she gets to know them. Nevertheless, she hopes to get rich through sales of mobile homes built to her design.

In what order should she undertake the following steps? Give a reason for each decision you make as you complete the table below.

A Hire a production manager.
B Select a site for the factory.
C Advertise the product on TV.
D Purchase the materials needed to build the product.
E Associate with an entrepreneur.
F Obtain a line of credit and issue shares.
G Conduct some market research.
H Engage workers for the factory.

STEP	LETTER	REASON
1	G	determine if it really could sell, and to whom
2	E	get advice, maybe partnership
3	F	get money to do A,B,C,D,H,
4	A	to start production process
5	B	''
6	D	''
7	H	''
8	C	to spread awareness of the product

4. You are considering setting up a butter factory in the Granby area. As a thinking entrepreneur your first step will be:

(A) to commission studies of the market for dairy products in the Montréal area.

(B) to buy herds of cattle in the Eastern Townships.

(C) to purchase modern equipment for your factory.

(D) to hire a plant manager.

Give a reason for your choice.

_____

_____

28

Operating a business

OUTLINE

To be successful and profitable a *business* has to be organized in as efficient a manner as possible. In the smallest businesses this can be done by the entrepreneur alone, but in most other companies this is achieved through dividing up the responsibilities. There is a **division of labour** and each of the various departments specializes in a certain aspect of the operation.

Administration
- oversees and coordinates the total operations of the company
- plans, organizes, leads, and evaluates the performance of the whole organization
- the **chairman** and the **board of directors** set policy and make major decisions
- the **president** or **general manager** is responsible for the day-to-day operations of the company. He/she may be assisted by an **executive committee**.

Administration usually divides the responsibilities for operations into manageable segments. Each department falls under the direction of a **manager** or a **vice-president** in the case of larger companies.

Most companies have the following departments:
Purchasing
- to obtain all supplies needed for making the product at the best prices and with the required quality

Production
- the **plant manager** ensures that the workers use the equipment efficiently to produce quality goods
- responsible for maintenance of equipment, quality control, work schedule, rate of production

Finance
- the **controller** *(sometimes spelled **comptroller**)* is in charge of this department
- ensures that the company has adequate and sustained financing at all times
- raises capital from banks, personal investors, and by issuing securities
- seeks government subsidies when they are available
- establishes a line of credit for the short-term requirements of the company *(payroll, accounts payable, taxes, etc.)*
- makes long-term projections about money needed to finance growth and replacement of capital goods

Human Resources (Personnel)
- the **human resources manager** must know and meet the labour requirements of the company
- hires workers, trains or retrains staff, evaluates performance, fires or lays off workers
- seeks to maintain high morale and motivation among the work force
- negotiates a collective agreement if the workers are unionized

Marketing (Sales)
- the **marketing and sales manager** is responsible for building and maintaining product sales
- conducts market research to establish consumer preferences and find new outlets for the product
- identifies segments of the market where product is selling well and areas where sales are poor
- arranges advertising campaigns
- maintains a network for sales and distribution of the product

1. Complete the **organization chart** *(sometimes called an **organigramme** in Québec)* to illustrate the structure of a typical business.

Name each department and also give the title of the person responsible for its operations.

> **STOCKHOLDERS**

elect

> **DIRECTORS**
> headed by the
> *Chairman*

They make decisions about policy and distribution of profits.

appoint

> *President*
>
> the salaried, responsible
> head of business operations

appoints

VICE-PRESIDENT in charge of *Purchasing*	VICE-PRESIDENT in charge of *Finance*	VICE-PRESIDENT in charge of *Marketing*	VICE-PRESIDENT in charge of *Production*

2. Talk to a relation or a friend to tell you about the organizational structure of the business where they work. What questions will you ask to check if the structure is similar to the one described above?

_____

_____

_____

_____

_____

3. In each of the following cases the company is facing a problem. Which part of the organization has the prime responsibility for dealing with the problem? Give a reason for your answer.

a) A major automobile manufacturer is having to make repairs to 20% of its new cars during their first six months of operation. Because these repairs fall under the terms of the manufacturer's guarantee, this is proving very costly to the company.

Department: _____

Reason: _____

_____

b) Faberski products are selling well, but the company cannot increase production since suppliers will not provide any more raw materials until all outstanding bills have been paid.

Department: _____

Reason: _____

_____

c) Glamorglo Inc. recently introduced what it believes to be an exciting new line of cosmetics. The products are sitting on the shelves of retail stores and there have been very few re-orders.

Department: _____

Reason: _____

_____

d) There is a lot of grumbling among the staff at Browning Office Supply Co.. People are complaining about wide variations in pay scales and the lack of a clear promotion policy. There is talk of forming a union.

Department: _____

Reason: _____

_____

e) Because of a declining market for private executive jets Jones Aircraft Corporation switched its plant to producing fine quality furniture. Many of the workers do not like their new jobs, quality is mostly poor, and sales have been disastrous to date.

Department: _____

Reason: _____

_____

Business efficiency

OUTLINE
Criteria for business efficiency

To make a profit a business has to be operated efficiently and its workers and plant need to be productive. How are **profitability** and **productivity** determined?

Profitability

Profit is the reward the entrepreneur gets for taking the risk in setting up a business. It is the difference between the *total revenue from sales* and the *total costs of production*.

TOTAL REVENUE **from sales**	**minus**	**TOTAL COSTS** **of production**	**=**	**PROFIT** *(This could be a **loss**.)*

The *costs of production* can be divided into:
- **fixed costs** which cannot be avoided no matter how big or small the production is. They include rent, interest payments, insurance premiums, administrative costs, and salaries of permanent employees.
- **variable costs** which change with the rate of production. They include the cost of materials, the cost of power *(electricity, gas, oil)*, wages of production workers, transportation costs.

The **gross profit** *(total revenue minus total costs)* does not all go to the entrepreneur. It is usually divided among:
- taxes paid to governments
- dividends paid to shareholders
- reinvestment in new equipment, expansion of production capacity, research and development (R&D)
- bonuses to the employees as a reward for increased productivity. (This is a small but growing trend.)

Profit can be justified on several grounds:
- It motivates entrepreneurs to take risks and to work hard at successfully combining the factors of production.
- It is an indicator of success. High cost competitors are forced to find ways of producing more efficiently or be driven out of business.
- It encourages people to invest in companies.
- It allows companies to finance their own growth and provide more jobs and better products.

Productivity

Productivity is a measure of the effectiveness of an individual, a team, or a company. It compares the total amount produced *(output)* with the amount of resources *(labour, capital, materials)* used in making the product *(input)*. The result has to be compared with previous results for the same company or with current results of other competing companies to have any real meaning.

<u>**OUTPUT of goods and/or services**</u> **INPUT of resources**	**=**	**PRODUCTIVITY**

If a fairly large quantity of output *(goods and services)* is produced using a fairly small quantity of input *(resources)*, then productivity is high. If the opposite holds true, then productivity is low.

Obviously, businesses seek to attain as much output as possible while reducing input to its lowest reasonable level. This can be achieved in a variety of ways:
- using the latest technology to reduce costs and/or improve quality e.g. robots, computers, irradiation
- training workers to become highly skilled specialists, retraining workers to up-date their skills
- finding new ways of combining resources to increase output and/or quality
- engaging in research and development (R&D)
- improving the working environment
- downsizing or rationalizing *(reducing)* the work force

TERMS

Explain these terms in your own words:

profit _____

productivity _____

APPLICATION

1. a) List the following items under the appropriate heading in the table below.

    b) Determine whether the store has made a profit over the month. How much?

THE VILLAGE SKI SHOP

Rent	$600	Sales of ski equipment	$2 900	Electricity	$60
Heating	$150	Revenue from ski school	$4 200	Telephone	$50
Goods in stock	$1 800	Sales of ski fashions	$1 500	Advertising	$240
Salaries	$5 100	Repairs to customers' equipment	$900	Interest on loans	$450

REVENUE	COSTS
$	$
$	$
$	$
$	$
$	$
$	$
$	$
$	$
TOTAL $	TOTAL $

2.   Use the data provided in the table to answer the following questions.

PETE'S PIZZA PARLOUR

Daily output $	Fixed costs $	Variable costs $	Revenue $
50	100	60	150
60	100	65	165
70	100	70	200
80	100	75	230
90	100	75	275
100	100	80	275

a)   What is the break-even point in this example?   _____

b)   At what point does Pete begin to make a profit?   _____

c)   At what point does he make his maximum profit?   _____

3. Three companies decide to publish a book about a famous rock star. Each is sure that his fans will eagerly buy its product. Look at the data in the table:

COMPANY	PRODUCT	PRODUCTION COSTS	PRICE PER UNIT	QUANTITY SOLD
A	Hard cover, glossy photos	$48 000	$25	2 100
B	Paper back, black & white photos	$21 000	$5	6 800
C	Soft cover, some colour photos	$45 000	$7	8 950

Calculate the profit made by each company. Which company made the greatest profit?

Profit made: Company A $_____   Company B $_____   Company C $_____

The most profitable is: _____

4. The office manager of the ABC Company has to make a decision.

Currently there are ten workers in the office. They are each paid $500 a week. Eight use Xtaq computers that are in good condition but two computers need to be replaced at a cost of $2500 each. Fixed costs are $450 a week.

A sales representative has explained the technical advantages of the new high-tech Wunderbar word processor. Three operators could do the same volume as the ten current employees using Xtaq computers. The standard wage for this grade of word processor operators is $750 a week. The equipment would cost $17 000 to buy and about $500 a week to operate.

a) Which system is more productive?   _____

b) Which system has higher set-up costs?   _____

c) Which system is more profitable over the course
   of one year (52 weeks)?   _____

5. A teenage disco club in the Montréal area has been hiring a DJ to supply music. The new owner believes that the club can be more attractive if he hires a local band to supply music. Study the data below and decide whether or not the business is more efficient as a result of the change.

JULY (Music supplied by a DJ)		AUGUST(Music supplied by a band)	
Input		*Input*	
Operating costs	$1 000	Operating costs	$1 000
Refreshments	$800	Refreshments	$2 500
Salary for DJ	$1 600	Salary for band	$7 000
Output		*Output*	
500 customers @ $3	$1 500	2 100 customers @ $5	$10 500
Sale of refreshments	$2 000	Sale of refreshments	$5 000

a) Is the new set-up more productive? Give a reason for your reply.

_____

_____

b) Is the new set-up more profitable? Give a reason for your reply.

_____

_____

6. "Increased productivity does not only result in higher profits for the business; it also produces benefits for society as a whole."

Consider this statement and then list some reasons to support it.

_____

_____

_____

_____

_____

_____

_____

_____

7. Consult the business section in newspapers and magazines or watch business programmes on TV. Try to find examples of companies that are both productive and profitable. Ascertain the reason(s) for the company's success.

Note your findings in the table below so that you can share your research with others.

NAME OF COMPANY	REASON(S) FOR SUCCESS

The role of private enterprises

OUTLINE

A **private enterprise** is an economic organization in which individuals own the capital resources. These capital resources are used to produce goods or services for private profit. Private enterprises take the form of **individual proprietorships, partnerships**, or **corporations**. Most of Canada's productive capacity is operated by private enterprise and financed by private capital.

Individual proprietorship

- Is a business established by an individual entrepreneur who finances the business and makes all decisions related to it. Thus it is easy to make decisions quickly. On the other hand, the entrepreneur may be forced to make decisions in areas where he/she has little expertise.
- The owner usually works in the business which can be involved in production, retailing, or providing a service. The hours of work may be very long especially when the business is being started.
- The size is often limited by the amount of capital which an individual is able to raise, so most individual proprietorships tend to be small businesses e.g. a farm, a machine shop, a boutique, a corner store, a dentist, an accountant.
- The owner enjoys all the profits or sustains all losses. He/she has **unlimited liability** *(If the owner cannot pay his debts, his bank accounts, home and other assets may be seized by his creditors.).*
- Since he/she operates in a competitive market each individual proprietor has little effect on establishing prices and little influence on the market.
- Individual proprietorships are easy to set up. The name of the company is **registered** so that no other business may use it. The business ceases to exist on the death of the owner or when he/she decides to go out of business.

Partnership

- Is an economic organization in which **two or more people** join together to form a business.
- The terms of the partnership are contained in an oral or written agreement. To withdraw, one must obtain permission from the other partner or partners. The partnership may have to be dissolved if one partner withdraws or dies.
- The capital is raised by the partners. Each shares in the profits or helps to sustain the losses. There is **unlimited liability**.
- Decision-making and workload are usually shared by the partners. The size and productivity of a partnership can exceed those of an individual proprietorship because there are more people and more expertise. Examples are legal firms, accounting firms, some medical groups, some retail stores, repair services.
- A single partnership has little effect on establishing prices or influencing the market.

Corporation

- Is an economic unit which is owned by a number of people called **shareholders** or **stockholders**.
- The shareholders have **limited liability** *(This means that the financial liability of the shareholders cannot exceed the amount of money they invested in the company.)*
- A corporation functions as a legal individual apart from the people who own or control it. It can sue, be sued, own property, and enter into contracts.
- The **promoters** *(the people who want to form a corporation)* must obtain a provincial or federal **charter** which grants permission to establish the corporation. Becoming incorporated is costly but the corporation can then add INC. *(Incorporated)* or LTD. *(Limited)* after its name.
- Having received a charter, the promoters sell securities to the public to finance the activities of the corporation.

   The **main types of securities** are:
   - **common shares** - A common shareholder is considered to be a part owner of the corporation and usually has voting privileges which permit some say in the control of company policy. The holder is paid a yearly **dividend** *(or share of the profits)* in proportion to the number of shares held - provided the company has made a profit!
   - **preferred shares** - A preferred shareholder is also a part owner of the corporation, but normally does not have any voting rights in the election of the board of directors. A **fixed dividend** is promised to be paid each year, but this can be waived by the board of directors.
   - **bonds** - A bondholder lends money to the corporation at a specified rate of interest for a specified period of time. The bondholder is considered to be just a lender so there are no voting privileges.

(*"Blue-chip shares"* are those issued by established, successful companies which make regular profits. They are usually high-priced and considered a safe investment.)

- Profits are used first to pay the interest due to *bondholders*. Secondly *preferred shareholders* are paid. *Common shareholders* are the last to be paid. Thus, investing in common shares carries more risk than does holding the other two types of securities. However, if profits are high, the value of the common shares will rise and the dividends paid to common shareholders can exceed the dividends paid to preferred shareholders or the amount of interest paid to bondholders. (Moreover, the owner can make a capital gain by selling shares when their price is higher than their cost.)
- Minority shareholders *(those with a small number of shares)* are often at the mercy of majority shareholders *(those with a large block of shares)* who may impose policies beneficial to themselves. Large blocks of shares are often owned by insurance companies, pension fund administrators, mutual fund investors, and banks.
- *Corporations* can raise large amounts of money by the sale of securities so they can undertake a major role in the production of goods. Some corporations grow to a large size and this allows them to influence prices and market conditions.
- *Corporations* can outlive their founders and shareholders so they have continuity from one generation to another. Shares are offered on the public stock exchange.
- People with various amounts of capital can invest in corporations through stock exchanges or brokers without having to set up their own businesses.
- *Corporations* suffer from double taxation: they pay taxes on their profits before declaring a dividend and then shareholders have to pay individual taxes on their share of the profits.

TERMS

Use your own words to distinguish between these terms:

limited liability and **unlimited liability**

"Limited liability" means _____

_____

"Unlimited liability" means _____

_____

shareholder and **bondholder**

"Shareholder" means _____

_____

"Bondholder" means _____

_____

APPLICATION

1. Complete the table to compare and contrast the three types of securities.

Type of security	Part owner of the corporation	Right to vote for the Board of Directors	Financial return on investment	Order of payment of profits
Bonds	NO			
Preferred shares			FIXED DIVIDEND	
Common shares		YES *(if voting shares)*		

2. Complete the table to compare and contrast the three types of private enterprises.

TYPE	INDIVIDUAL PROPRIETORSHIP	PARTNERSHIP	CORPORATION
Number of owners	1	2 +	1 +
Amount of liability	unlimited	unlimited	limited
Average size			
Who gets profits?	owner	partners	Shareholders
Who makes decisions?	owner	partners	"
How is capital raised?	given by owner or loan	given by partners or loans	shares & stock
How easy is it to set up?	easy peasy	little harder	$$
Give some examples in your area.			

3. Compare the advantages and disadvantages of an individual proprietorship.

ADVANTAGES	DISADVANTAGES

4. Compare the advantages and disadvantages of a corporation.

ADVANTAGES	DISADVANTAGES

5. Select the following statement which best defines a **charter**?

(A) A document which establishes credit for a corporation.

(B) Written permission given by the board of directors to the promoters to establish the corporation.

(C) A document given by the government which instructs the promoters as to how capital may be raised for the corporation.

(D) Written permission issued by a provincial or federal government which permits the setting up of a corporation by its promoters.

6. The **major responsibility** of the board of directors is:

(A) to establish policies for the corporation.

(B) to hire managers for the company.

(C) to encourage shareholders to invest more money in the corporation.

(D) to conduct the day to day business of the company.

The role of cooperatives

OUTLINE

A **cooperative** is a business organization set up for the mutual benefit and interest of all its **members**.

Normally a cooperative is formed by the people living in a community or region. (It is usually referred to as "the co-op".) They set up the cooperative to protect themselves against high interest rates, exploitation, and corrupt or unfair business practices. The usual goal is to offer goods and/or services to members at more reasonable rates. The human aspect of providing service to the members is the major concern of the cooperative rather than making a high profit.

Distinguishing features of a cooperative

- Control of the cooperative is in the hands of the **members** *(the people who use it)*. It operates on a one member - one vote basis. Membership is open to all and is voluntary. All members may participate in the election of the executive committee.
- It provides goods and services to its members at a reduced rate or even at cost plus handling charges.
- Capital is invested for the purpose of providing goods and services at a reduced cost rather than for the expected return on investment in the form of dividends. If there is a surplus arising out of the cooperative's operations, it is distributed equitably among the members according to their frequency of use of the services.
- The members are not liable for the debts of the cooperative. They are liable to lose only the value of their membership share. Because of this limited liability, members may come and go without affecting the existence of the cooperative.
- Although democratically controlled, cooperatives provide for the training of good managers. They also provide for the education of their members, employees, and the general public.
- Capacity for growth is limited because each cooperative serves a relatively small group. Many are **affiliated** *(have a close association)* with other cooperatives outside the area on a regional, provincial, national, or even international basis. This affiliation can be in the form of a **federation** or a **confederation**.

Types of cooperatives

- **Production and marketing cooperatives** handle one or more products which the members raise, cultivate, catch, or make for sale to someone else. Services may include processing, grading, packaging, labelling, and advertising. Examples: dairy co-op, wheat producers' co-op, fishermen's co-op, handicraft makers' co-op

- **Consumer and purchasing cooperatives** purchase raw materials and supplies needed by members in large quantities at reduced rates and then distribute them to members at reduced prices. Examples: groceries, building materials, fertilizers, machinery, fishing equipment.

- **Service cooperatives** offer something for the members that requires specialized skills and equipment. Examples: day-care facilities, funeral co-ops, some health organizations, insurance co-ops, housing co-ops.

- **Workers cooperatives** are organized so that all the employees of an enterprise may participate in owning and controlling the policies of their business. Example: printing, paper mill.

- **Financial cooperatives** offer lending, saving, and chequing services to their members. They compete with banks and trust companies by offering parallel services. Examples: *caisses populaires* and credit unions.

Cooperatives are more numerous in Québec than in other regions of Canada. The Canadian cooperative movement began in Québec when Alphonse Desjardins established the first *caisse populaire* at Lévis in 1900.

APPLICATION

1. Complete the chart to compare and contrast a cooperative and a corporation.

	COOPERATIVE	CORPORATION
Who owns it?		
How can you become an owner?		
Who controls it?		
Who manages it?		
What is its main purpose?		
How is capital raised?		
How are profits distributed?		
How much liability is there for losses?		
Is there a limit to size?		

2. Name some cooperatives in your district. Why was each formed?

_____

_____

_____

_____

_____

_____

The role of publicly-owned enterprises

OUTLINE

Publicly-owned enterprises are businesses in which capital resources are owned by a government (federal, provincial, or municipal). They can be grouped into these principal types:

Public services

- Some government undertakings are **services** provided for the well-being of the community. They are not designed to make a profit. They are paid for partly through user fees *(bus fares, licences, camping fees, etc.)* but mainly from taxes. Examples: public transportation, museums, recreation facilities, schools, health facilities, parks, research laboratories, Employment Insurance Commission.
- These services are under the direct control of the government.

Public enterprises

- These are called ***sociétés d'État*** in Québec (e.g. Hydro-Québec, Société des Alcools du Québec, Caisse de dépôt et placement) and **crown corporations** throughout Canada (e.g. Canada Post, CBC). Most were set up in sectors of the economy where private enterprise was experiencing difficulties or was reluctant to invest.
- They have a certain degree of **autonomy** to operate without direct government interference. Each has a board of directors. However, they are ultimately accountable to Parliament or a provincial legislature for their conduct of affairs.
- They are financed through government grants, loans, and by borrowing in the private sector. If the crown corporation is operating at a loss, the government usually finds the necessary funds to keep it functioning.
- All or most of the shares are owned by the government. If there is a profit, it goes to the government if it is not used for reinvestment purposes.
- They function as independent legal "persons" and enjoy limited liability. They can borrow money - usually backed by a guarantee from the government. They pay taxes.

Mixed enterprises

- These are partly owned by the government and partly by private investors. The government has the right to appoint some members to the board of directors.
- Sometimes the government is trying to help an ailing enterprise by supplying some much needed capital which would otherwise be difficult to obtain.
- The *Caisse de dépôt et placement du Québec* is a major investor in many large corporations. It invests the money collected for government pension funds and accident insurance. It owns large blocks of shares in companies such as Domtar, Noranda, Alcan, Canadian Pacific, Gaz Métropolitain, and BCE. In these cases the managers of the *Caisse de dépôt* are just trying to get a good return on funds being held by the government.

Origins and recent trends

Most publicly-owned enterprises were set up by the government using public funds. In some cases the government felt it necessary to take over private enterprises because they were failing and the politicians considered them essential for the national good. In a few cases the government acquired the companies by **nationalization** *(passing a law forcing the company to sell its assets to the government at a price considered fair by the government)*.

In recent years there has been a tendency for governments to **divest** themselves of publicly-owned enterprises. Many crown corporations persistently lose money. Some business people believe this is mainly due to poor management. They claim that **privatization** *(a return to the private sector)* will make the companies more productive and profitable. Normally, only successful and profitable crown corporations are bought by private investors.

TERMS

Explain these terms in your own words:

public service

_____

_____

crown corporation

_____

_____

nationalization

_____

_____

APPLICATION

1. The table below lists some of the sociétés d'État belonging to the government of Québec. Explain the reason for setting each up.

Hydro-Québec	
Société des alcools du Québec	
Loto-Québec	
Télé-Québec	
Sidérurgie du Québec (SIDBEC)	

2. Name some important crown corporations belonging to the federal government of Canada.

    i _____

    ii _____

3. Name some formerly publicly-owned enterprises that have been returned to the private sector.

    i _____

    ii _____

Small and medium-sized businesses

OUTLINE

So far we have classified businesses according to their **ownership** and **organization**, but they can also be classified according to their **size**. Size can be measured by the number of employees and by the amount of capital invested in the company. Even so, the *Ministère de l'Industrie et du Commerce du Québec* finds it useful to have different scales for businesses engaged in manufacturing and businesses involved in the commerce and service sectors.

MANUFACTURING SECTOR		Size	COMMERCE & SERVICE SECTOR	
Number of employees	*Investment capital $*		*Number of employees*	*Investment capital $*
1 - 4	under 200 000	CRAFT SHOP	1 - 3	under 200 000
5 - 49	under 1 500 000	SMALL	4 - 10	under 1 000 000
50 - 199	under 6 000 000	MEDIUM	11 - 30	under 5 000 000
200 - 499	under 15 000 000	LARGE	31 and over	over 5 000 000
500 and over	over 15 000 000	VERY LARGE		

SOURCE: Ministère de l'Industrie et du Commerce du Québec

Over 90% of the business establishments in Canada belong to the small and medium categories. They employ about half of the work force and produce about a third of the GDP. Between 1979 and 1989 they generated 2.1 million new jobs - 81% of all new jobs in Canada.

Characteristics of small and medium-sized businesses

- They produce for the local and regional market rather than for the national market.
- Many are in retailing and the service sector e.g. small stores, service stations, repair services, landscaping, carpentry
- Some manufacture parts for larger companies located in the region e.g. windows, doors, metal fittings, fences, cabinets for home building contractors.
- The owner usually participates in the business and works closely with the employees.
- Many fail in the early years: 35% in their first year, 50% within the first two years, 95% within ten years

Advantages of small and medium-sized businesses

- They favour more personalized relationships between management and production staff and between the company and its customers. In cases where the business is long-established the loyalty of the employees is usually strong.
- Management frequently comes from the local area and is thoroughly familiar with changes in the conditions of supply and demand. They are often shrewd enough to survive on the limited resources of one area.
- Major decisions are made locally, therefore the effects on the local area and its inhabitants are of prime concern.
- It is easier to adapt schedules and products to fit the exact requirements of customers.
- Smallness and flexibility allow them to be innovative, to find new methods or inventions to produce more efficiently. In some cases employees suggest how the process can become more productive. Innovation usually begins on a small scale.
- Most new jobs are now created in this sector. They are mostly **tertiary activities** *(those which provide services)* such as restaurants, hotels, advertising, financial services, transportation.
- They can be set up in small towns and in rural areas where there is an urgent need for more jobs.

Disadvantages of small and medium-sized businesses

- Management may not have all the necessary skills and experience required for all aspects of the business. There may not be enough volume of business to justify hiring other managers.
- It is sometimes difficult to attract specialized labour and senior managers with the necessary training and experience in the latest technologies to come to work in small establishments away from the large cities.
- Adequate financing can be a problem, especially for businesses that are not firmly established. Small businesses often find it too expensive to issue securities to raise money so they have to rely mainly on personal savings, investments by friends, and a line of credit or a short-term loan from the bank. They have few assets to offer a security for loans. They may be forced to pay higher rates of interest. As far as possible small and medium-sized businesses try to be self-financing.
- Small businesses face stiff competition if there are also large companies in the same line of business. Large competitors can obtain materials more cheaply from suppliers and they can lower prices more to obtain a contract.
- Their volume of business may be small so fixed costs form a relatively high proportion of the total cost. This reduces their competitiveness and their profit margin.
- Having to comply with government regulations and complete official paperwork including collecting GST can be a burden to small businesses.

Government assistance

- Because small and medium-sized businesses are important creators of new job opportunities, and also because they offer a diversity of economic activities in regions where growth is needed, both the federal and the provincial governments offer various types of assistance.
- **credit** or **lower interest rates** backed by the government
- **subsidies** to set up a plant and to train workers
- **consulting services** for the management; research facilities in government laboratories
- **tax rebates** to encourage investors to buy shares of these companies (Québec Stock Savings Plan gives investors favourable tax treatment.)

APPLICATION

1. In Québec a small or medium-sized business is often referred to as a "PME". Find out what PME stands for.

    _____

2. Some new jobs are opening up in a small company which currently has only 15 employees. The types of work being offered appeal to you so you are considering making an application. However, there is also a possibility of getting a job on the production line of a large company. You have a decision to make.

    a) List three advantages of taking a job at the small company.

    i _____

    ii _____

    iii _____

    b) List three disadvantages of working at the small company.

    i _____

    ii _____

    iii _____

3. List examples of businesses found in your local area according to their size. If necessary, use the yellow pages in the phone book for names. For each business, indicate the nature of the product or service.

NAME OF BUSINESS	PRODUCT or SERVICE
SMALL BUSINESSES	
1	
2	
3	
4	
5	
6	
7	
8	
9	
10	
12	
13	
14	
15	
MEDIUM-SIZED BUSINESSES	
1	
2	
3	
4	
5	
6	
7	
LARGE BUSINESSES	
1	
2	
3	
4	
5	

Large companies

OUTLINE

In the manufacturing sector a company is considered large when it has 200 and more employees and a capital investment of more than $6 000 000. In the commercial and service sectors businesses with 31 or more employees and over $5 000 000 in assets are considered large.

While not numerous (less than 6%), large companies are responsible for more than half the production and provide many jobs. In recent years many large companies have restructured their labour force. This **"down-sizing"** has resulted in many large lay-offs of workers from their jobs.

Advantages of large companies

- It is relatively easy for them to raise capital. Most are publicly-held private corporations whose shares are traded on the stock exchange. They were originally financed by issuing securities *(stocks and bonds)*. From time to time additional financing is achieved through issuing treasury shares, new bonds, or by selling rights *(a privilege granted to shareholders to buy additional shares directly from the company)* and warrants *(certificates granting the holder the right to purchase securities at a stipulated price within a specified period of time)*.
- They can negotiate the lowest prices for supplies. Sometimes they own the sources of their main supplies.
- If there is a small number of companies in the same line of business, they can form a **cartel** *(an association of independent producers who work together to control production, distribution, and prices for their products or services)* and thus have a strong influence on setting market prices.
- They are well-known and offer more chances for advancement, so they are attractive to managers and specialized workers. They can afford to hire the best minds to develop or improve their products.
- They can afford to purchase the latest equipment and engage in costly research and development (R&D) projects.
- They can afford to conduct expensive advertising campaigns on a national scale. If necessary, they can engage in price wars with their competitors to gain a larger share of the market or protect their own interests.

Disadvantages of large companies

- Their work force is large and can become impersonal. Workers and managers get switched from plant to plant.
- The work force is normally unionized and this can lead to union-management conflicts. A detailed labour contract and a complex management structure may make it harder to adapt and be responsive to changing market conditions.
- Their size and responsibility may make them less responsive to local needs and the special requirements of particular customers. Administrators tend to be moved around frequently so they may not feel strong ties to the community. However, most large companies try to be "good corporate citizens" and support the community in which the plant is located through generous donations to charities, sponsorship of teams and cultural activities, and offering bursaries and prizes to aid students.
- Only a few large companies are owned and controlled by Quebecers or other Canadians (e.g. Molson-O'Keefe, Power Corporation). Because much of the investment capital has traditionally come from the United States and Western Europe, and nowadays also from Japan and Hong Kong, many of our large industries are foreign owned and controlled.

Government aid to large companies

- Large companies are very important to the economy of the area in which they are located; not only do they provide several hundred **direct jobs**, they also lead to two or three times that number of **indirect jobs** in feeder industries and in the commerce and service sectors. Thus, governments are willing to grant large multi-million dollar subsidies or low or interest-free loans to large corporations to persuade them to locate or remain in a certain district.
- Some large companies that have run into financial difficulties and find it hard to raise new money by selling stocks and bonds turn to the governments for help.

Global / Multinational corporations

- To be called **global** or **multinational**, a corporation must have a subsidiary company in at least one other country besides the one where the parent company is located. Example: Alcan has its headquarters in Montreal but it owns other subsidiary companies in several countries.
- Most multinationals are headquartered in the United States, Western Europe, or Japan.
- Multinationals supply us with many of the products we use every day: e.g. cars, petroleum products, processed food, detergents, paper and packaging, electrical and electronic equipment.
- Characteristics include sales revenues exceeding a billion dollars a year, profits in excess of 100 million dollars a year, and assets worth more than a billion dollars.
- Their size can be awesome. The largest global corporations such as ExxonMobil, General Motors, and IBM earn an annual sales revenue greater than the GDP of many of the world's smaller countries. They can transfer vast amounts of capital and many employees to host countries so they have a very strong influence wherever they locate. Their economic influence has been felt for many years around the world.

APPLICATION

1. Give four examples of multinational companies that supply some of the day to day needs of your family.

    i_____   ii_____

    ii_____   iv_____

2. a) Name three examples of multinational companies based in Québec.

    i_____ ii_____ iii_____

   b) Name three examples of multinational companies based in the rest of Canada.

    i_____ ii_____ iii_____

3. Some Canadians are concerned about the extent of foreign investment and control over our manufacturing sector.

    a) Refer to a listing of the largest companies in Canada including Québec. Determine which industries are particularly under the control of foreign companies.

    _____

    _____

    b) What are the advantages and disadvantages for Canadians?

    _____

    _____

    _____

Integration of companies

OUTLINE

Many individual corporations control or attempt to gain control of the markets in which they operate. They try to combine or integrate separate companies into a single integrated corporation.

The reasons for this are varied:
- a desire to expand and increase profits
- to benefit more fully from the advantages of mass production
- to produce an end product without dependence on other companies
- to meet special capital or labour requirements

Because large corporations buy other companies to merge or join them into their organization, the term **merger** is used to describe the **takeover** of one company by another.

Forms of integration

- **vertical integration** consists of a company controlling the production process from beginning to end, from the raw material to the finished product.

  EXAMPLES
  - *Alcan* owns its bauxite mines, its shipping company, its smelters, and its sales and distribution network
  - *Domtar* controls logging operations, companies producing the chemicals used in making paper, newsprint mills, fine paper and wrapping paper mills, and has sales divisions for the domestic and overseas markets.
  - *Petro-Canada* owns oil wells, searches for new deposits, operates refineries, runs a chain of gas stations, sells home heating oil, and conducts research.

- **horizontal integration** consists of combining companies making the same or similar products, or offering the same or similar services. This allows certain **economies of scale** in management, bulk buying, etc. It may lead to market domination and subsequently control over prices.

  EXAMPLES
  - *Quebecor Inc.* is a media group. *Quebecor World Inc.* controls the world's largest group of commercial printing companies. It publishes 8 regional daily newspapers across Canada (including the *Journal de Montréal*) and 160 weekly newspapers, in addition to numerous magazines. It controls several book publishing companies. *Quebecor Media Inc.* controls a television station *(TVQ)*, a cable company *(Vidéotron)*, internet services *(Canoe)*, retail stores for CDs, DVDs *(Archambault)*, and video-rental stores *(Super-Club Vidéotron)*
  - *The Bay*, a large retail company with a cross-Canada chain of stores acquired control of Simpson's Ltd., *Zellers Inc.*, and *K-Mart Inc.*- three other retail chains.

- **conglomerates** are created by grouping companies involved in independent activities. This kind of integration minimizes the risk of a downturn in one sector of the economy. If one company fails or does poorly, profits from the other companies in the conglomerate cover the loss or supply funds to cover operating costs.

  EXAMPLES
  - *Canadian Pacific Limited (CP)* which was originally a transportation company now controls companies involved in mining, communications, hotels, etc.
  - *Power Corporation* is a large Québec-based conglomerate with activities in several fields.

TERMS

Explain this term in your own words:

merger / takeover

_____

_____

APPLICATION·

1. What forms of integration are exemplified by the following organization charts?

    a) _____

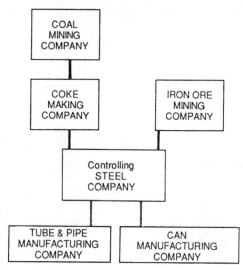

    b) _____

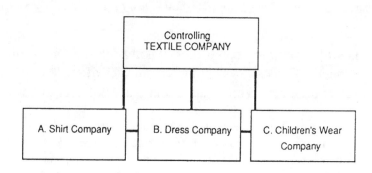

2. A Canadian company has expanded both vertically and horizontally during the past ten years. This company is now:

    a multinational? ____   a conglomerate? ____   a cartel? ____

3. Several small mining companies in northern Québec do not have sufficient funds to continue exploration and drilling. A large company in the area makes offers to purchase these companies. The offers are accepted. This is an example of:

    vertical integration? ____   horizontal integration? ____   a conglomerate? ____

4. The Canadian Shoe Corporation already owns Kumfy Shoes Ltd., ABC Footwear Inc., and Sports Shoes Ltd.. If it attempts to merge Dark's Shoes Ltd., an independent company, into its group of companies, this would be an example of:

    a conglomerate? ____   horizontal integration? ____   vertical integration? ____

Module 3

HUMAN RESOURCES

OBJECTIVES

3.1   *Establish the relationship between human resources and production.*

3.2   *Describe the structures and mechanisms of the labour system.*

As you know, there are three factors of production: natural resources, capital resources, and human resources. This module concentrates on the human resources.

The workers at any level in the production chain form the human resources. It could be an entrepreneur - the individual with the ideas and the drive, the willingness to take economic risks in new business ventures. It could be an executive or manager who has to make daily decisions affecting the operations of the company. Or it could be a production worker, that important individual who turns the product on a lathe, the driver trucking produce to market, the key-punch operator, or the salesperson.

You too will most probably be entering the labour force upon completion of your educational career. This module will help you to be better prepared for that time when you also become a "human resource" participating in the economy.

Characteristics of the labour force

OUTLINE
Definitions
- **work** = those activities that are carried out in the market for *pay* or *profit* and not the numerous non-market activities such as housework and volunteer work.

- **labour force** (sometimes called the **active population** or the **work force**) = the portion of the population 15 years of age and over which is employed or actively seeking work

- **employed** = those at work, or those who have a job but are not at work because of illness, disability, vacation, labour dispute, or other reason

- **unemployed** = those without work but who are available for employment and are actively seeking work

- **"hidden unemployed"** = those who wish to work but have given up looking for a job

- **employment rate** (sometimes called the **participation rate**) =

$$\frac{\text{Labour force}}{\text{Population 15 years of age and over}} \quad \text{x} \quad 100$$

- **unemployment rate** = $\dfrac{\text{Unemployed}}{\text{Labour force}}$ x   100

The following are **not** considered to be part of the labour force:
- full-time students in high school, college, or university
- persons aged 15 or over who do not wish to work
- full-time members of the Canadian armed forces
- inmates of institutions *(prisons, mental hospitals)*
- persons living on Indian reserves
- residents of the Yukon, the Northwest Territories, and Nunavut

Size and composition of the labour force
- **age**
  - About two-thirds of the total population are of working age (15+) but less than half of the population is in the labour force.
  - Most people in the 25-55 age bracket are in the labour force. There is a rapid drop off after age 55 because of retirement, illness, and inability to find work at this age. The official retirement age in Canada is 65 but many retire before their 65th birthday and some work beyond their 65th birthday.

- **sex**
  - Traditionally most men 25 years and over have been in the labour force. In the last decades the proportion of women in the labour force has been steadily increasing. In 1991, 60% of all women of working age were employed. Women formed 45% of the labour force in 1991.
  - Increasingly women assume roles once considered to be suitable for men only. Today there are female butchers, truck drivers, heavy equipment operators, lawyers, executives, etc.
  - The advent of many labour-saving devices for use in the home and the decrease in the size of families due to birth control methods have allowed more and more women to remain longer in the labour force or to return to full time employment once their children are older.
  - In more and more families women work because it is necessary to maintain the family's standard of living. It is becoming necessary to provide more and more daycare facilities for the young children of workers. In 1991, 68% of women with children at home had a job or were looking for one.

- **level of education**
  - Some workers are more highly educated, trained, or skilled than others. This affects their level of remuneration *(wages or salary)* and how much their services will be in demand.
  - It also is an important factor in determining the worker's type of responsibility. Workers with university education tend to work at conceptual jobs, those with CÉGEP qualifications only tend to find technical work, and those with no more than high school education tend to work at the production level.
  - The workers' level of education also affects the chance of being unemployed: 1 chance in 2 for high school drop-outs; 1 in 4 for those who only gain a high school leaving certificate. CÉGEP and university graduates have better chances of avoiding long-term unemployment.
  - Those with few skills and a low level of education find it most difficult to find and keep a job with a reasonable wage.
  - There are now more women graduates from Canadian universities than male graduates.

- **sectors of economic activity**
  - Workers can be categorized according to their sector of employment:

    Primary *(basic work)*
    - jobs concerned with the exploitation of natural resources before they are transformed into manufactured products. e.g. farmers, miners, loggers, fishermen, hunters and trappers.

    Secondary *(manufacturing)*
    - jobs that transform materials into finished products. e.g. textiles, furniture, electrical accessories. It includes all workers in the manufacturing and construction sectors. Goods are produced not services provided.

    Tertiary *(service sector)*
    - jobs in the service, commercial, financial and professional sectors. e.g. transportation, advertising, retailing, banking, government services, restaurants, entertainment, hotels. Services are provided but no goods are produced.

  - In 2001, the primary sector employed about 5% of the labour force; 20% were in the secondary sector. Nearly three-quarters (75%) were in the tertiary sector which was growing at the expense of the other two. With technological progress, machines replaced much human labour in the primary and secondary sectors. Now computers are taking the place of many workers in administrative and secretarial jobs in the tertiary sector. As Toffler said, there is a transition from "brute force" to "brain-based" employment.

APPLICATION

1. Country "Z" has a total population of 5 million people. 3 million are aged 15 and over. There are 2 million people in the labour force and half a million are unemployed.

   a) Calculate the number employed. _____

   b) Calculate the unemployment rate. _____

   c) Calculate the employment rate. _____

   d) Calculate the number who have chosen not to be part of the labour force. _____

2. Give examples of jobs in each of the three sectors:

   a) primary   i_____   ii_____

   iii_____   iv_____

   b) secondary   i_____   ii_____

   iii_____   iv_____

   c) tertiary   i_____   ii_____

   iii_____   iv_____

3. Which of the following are part of the labour force?

   a) Jean is 14 and she delivers newspapers each morning.   _____

   b) Frank worked as a plumber's helper for 2 years and now he is looking for
      a different job with more challenge.   _____

   c) Helga has three young children so she stays home to care for them.   _____

   d) Greg was in prison for three years but he is now out looking for a job.   _____

   e) Dorothy is a general in the Canadian Armed Forces.   _____

   f) Grace is 27 years old and she is learning to be a heart surgeon.   _____

   g) Phil works three days a week at a fast food restaurant.   _____

   h) Lisa was on EI for a year and is now receiving welfare payments,
      but she is still trying to find a job.   _____

4. Use the labels listed below to complete the diagram which illustrates how the population of a country
   can be divided up.

   Labels: POPULATION UNDER 15 YEARS   ACTIVE POPULATION
                  PEOPLE WITH JOBS   INACTIVE POPULATION
                  POPULATION 15 YEARS AND OVER   UNEMPLOYED

   ```
                          ┌─────────────────────┐
                          │  TOTAL POPULATION   │
                          └─────────────────────┘
           ┌──────────────┐              ┌──────────────────┐
           │              │              │                  │
           └──────────────┘              └──────────────────┘
              ┌──────────────┐        ┌──────────────────┐
              │              │        │                  │
              └──────────────┘        └──────────────────┘
                 ┌──────────────┐        ┌──────────────────┐
                 │              │        │                  │
                 └──────────────┘        └──────────────────┘
   ```

5. Susan has just finished high school. Believing in equal opportunities for women, she has applied for
   a job as a crane operator at a new construction site.

   Phil is 26 years old and is married with two young children. He worked as a crane operator for another
   construction company before it went out of business. He has also applied for the job.

   Phil got the job. Give reasons why he was preferred over Susan.

   _____

   _____

   _____

   _____

   _____

Unemployment

Unemployment is a persistent problem for some members of the labour force in our economy. There will always be some unemployment as there are always a few people who have left one job and are searching for something more attractive or better suited to their training and interests. Economists consider an **unemployment rate** of 4% or less to be "full employment". In recent years the unemployment rate in Québec has been over 10%. The average rate for young workers (15 to 24 age group) is much higher (about 20% at times). The rate for women averages higher than the rate for men.

Causes of unemployment
- Sometimes there is a recession in the economy (consumers buy less, production is cut back, fewer workers are needed, businesses close down).
- Canadian businesses are *not always competitive* with foreign suppliers whose prices are often lower.
- The education system is *not always preparing some young people adequately* for the conditions of today's job market.
- Workers are *not sufficiently mobile*; the unemployment rate is much higher in some regions.
- The workers born during the "baby boom" (now aged 40 to 55) have occupied their jobs for a long time and this makes it *difficult for younger workers to progress* up the ladder. For many years, fewer new jobs were created. This will change as the "baby boomers" retire.
- Canada has had one of the *poorer records for R&D (research and development)* among the industrialized countries. This has an impact on quality and innovations.
- Our *generous social system* provides employment insurance and welfare payments which discourage some people from looking seriously for work.
- Government *policies for reducing unemployment have often proven ineffective*. Many find it better to rely on their own initiatives to find another job.
- Our *cold winters* force some types of employment to cease operations until the milder weather returns.

Types of unemployment
- **Frictional unemployment** will always be present in a market economy. People who have been fired or people who have quit to seek a better job are really between jobs. This kind of unemployment is due to friction and is unavoidable. Indeed, it is desirable because the mobility of workers normally results in improvements and greater productivity.

- **Structural unemployment** results from redundancy. Because of changes in the market or through changing technology certain kinds of workers are no longer required. This is structural unemployment. As far as possible, the displaced workers need to be retrained to perform other tasks. As a result of rapid technological changes, more and more workers can expect to face structural unemployment. It has been forecast that most people will have five different jobs during their working career.

- **Seasonal unemployment** results from the seasonal changes affecting certain sectors. Fishing ceases in winter. Ski resorts close in spring.

- **Cyclical unemployment** is the type most feared by governments. In a mixed economy business experiences an *economic cycle* which has periods of prosperity followed by recession. In periods of prosperity demand is increasing, expectations are rising, and there are many employment opportunities. In a recession demand slackens, producers cut back, and fewer workers are needed. The worst situation occurs in a *depression* when the economy slows down considerably and the unemployment rate becomes unacceptably high. Then the public exerts great pressure on governments to find remedies and the total employment insurance budget becomes a big financial drain.

("Hidden unemployment" is a term referring to workers who are so discouraged that they have given up actively seeking a job. They are not counted among the unemployed in government statistics.)

Corrective measures

To combat unemployment governments have several possible strategies, but each tends to be costly.

- *Grant subsidies* to businesses to set up new ventures that will create new employment or maintain existing jobs. It often requires millions of dollars to create or maintain only a few permanent jobs. Many schemes produce only temporary jobs.

- *Reduce business taxes* to encourage expansion of industry and commerce. This results in some new jobs, but businesses often use their increased revenue to reduce their debt instead.

- *Reduce personal taxes* to encourage consumers to spend more and increase demand. This works to a degree, but in a recession people tend to be pessimistic and hold on to their extra money.

- *Encourage work-sharing* through working shorter hours or part-time. More people would have work, but many workers would earn less. Politicians tend to avoid this solution.

- *Improve confidence in the economy.* While everyone agrees on the goal, there is much disagreement about the method. Some want to move towards a pure market economy *(no government interference)*, others advocate more state control.

APPLICATION

1. Find out the current unemployment rate in Québec and Canada for each of the groups named in the table below. Rates for recent years are given in parentheses.

UNEMPLOYMENT RATES _____ (Add date)

Group	CANADA (2002) *(including Québec)*	QUÉBEC (2001)
All people in the labour force	(7.5%)	(8.5%)
Young people (15 to 19)	(20.2%)	(18.2%)
Men	(8.1%)	(9.0%)
Women	(7.1%)	(8.5%)

2. Find some current data about unemployment rates.
   a) Is the current trend in the unemployment rate up or down? _____

   b) What are its principal causes?

   i_____

   ii_____

   iii_____

3. Complete the chart below to compare and contrast the four main types of unemployment.

Type of unemployment	Cause	Possible solution(s)
SEASONAL		
FRICTIONAL		
STRUCTURAL		
CYCLICAL		

4. What type of unemployment is represented by each of the following examples?

a) Computers have replaced ten office workers at Gilson Co. _____

b) Department stores hire extra staff in the weeks before Christmas and then fire them in the new year. _____

c) Peter quit after an argument with the boss and is now looking for a job. _____

d) Workers at Giant Motors are laid off because of slow sales and a large inventory of unsold cars. _____

e) Telephone operators were replaced by automatic dialling equipment. _____

f) Joanna searched for a job for 15 months, but she gave up in frustration about a year ago. _____

5. What should governments do to reduce the high levels of unemployment among the 15 to 24 years age group. Note your suggestions below.

_____

_____

_____

_____

_____

The cost of labour

OUTLINE

Whenever we pay for a good or a service, some part of that payment must go towards the cost of labour. How much a worker is paid for his or her labour is determined by several factors.

The supply and demand for labour

- **Labour surplus** - If there are many workers seeking a limited number of jobs, employers are not inclined to pay high wages. This is particularly true where the jobs require little training or skill so any worker can be easily replaced.
- **Labour shortage** - If there are relatively few workers and several employers are eager to attract as many of them as possible to work in their plants, then wages will tend to be high. This is true of certain sports and entertainment stars. It also applies to some workers in high-tech industries.
- **High unemployment** - In a town with much unemployment, wages tend to be below average because workers are willing to accept less remuneration just to get a job.
- **Remote areas** - In an isolated region where workers with certain special skills are difficult to find, employers will pay very high wages just to attract the workers they need to move to the isolated work site.

Personal factors

- **Level of education** - In general, the longer one has attended school the higher will be the rate of pay. High school dropouts average low salaries, those with advanced university degrees tend to command the higher rates.
- **Sex** - In many jobs men are paid more than women for doing equivalent work. Though inequalities remain, equal pay for equivalent work is becoming increasingly common.
- **Experience and seniority** - Experienced workers are usually paid more because they are more skilled. Indeed for some jobs there are pay scales and the worker earns more each successive year till the top of the scale is reached. Very experienced workers may become supervisors or foremen and this results in higher pay.

Type of work

- **Responsibility** - Executives and managers earn high salaries. Airline pilots and heart surgeons are also highly paid. A skilled machinist making a jet engine or a computer programmer can expect fairly high wages. A bell-hop in a hotel or a cleaner is poorly paid because society does not consider their jobs require much skill nor carry much responsibility.
- **Degree of risk or unpleasantness** - Miners do risky work in difficult surroundings so their pay scales are high. Workers tending furnaces and pouring molten metal in steel mills also are well paid.

Place of work

- **Unionization** - If the workers at a plant are unionized, wages are probably higher than in an equivalent non-unionized plant. The union has negotiated a collective agreement which controls remuneration and working conditions. It negotiates with the company to arrive at an acceptable salary scale in relation to job skills and experience. Unskilled workers with no union protection are sometimes exploited and receive very poor wages.
- **Parity** - When there are several companies in the same line of business operating in the same region, they have to pay similar salaries. If one company pays much below the general level, its best employees will be tempted to go to work for its competitors. To avoid this situation, it has to pay comparable pay scales; in other words, its workers enjoy parity with those in similar establishments.
- **Isolation** - To persuade workers to accept jobs in the Far North or on oil rigs out at sea it is necessary to offer high wages.
- **Pay equity** Public service unions are now demanding and getting pay equity which aims to have fair treatment for workers with similar training and responsibilities even though they work in different fields. It is difficult to equate the work and pay scales for engineers, nurses, teachers and accountants. It is easier to grant equal pay to men and women working in the same field.

Role of governments

- In each province the government sets the **minimum wage rate** per hour to protect new and younger workers from exploitation.
- Governments negotiate or decree wage scales for their own employees. If the government pays well, private businesses are forced to pay more too.
- If wages are very low in some foreign countries and their low-priced goods are threatening to deprive Canadian workers of their jobs, the federal government can set **tariffs** *(customs duties)* and **quotas** *(import limits)* to protect our domestic industries.

Labour costs in industry

- The labour costs of businesses vary by the types and numbers of workers they employ. If industries are compared, they tend to fall into one of the following categories:

- **labour intensive industries** in which many people are employed in the production process. Labour costs are high in proportion to production value. They use a lot of human resources and relatively little capital and material resources.

- **capital intensive industries** in which few people are employed. Labour costs are low in relation to equipment, energy, and material costs. The costs of capital goods and materials are high in proportion to production value.

- Many industries are tending towards capital intensive development. The number of jobs will decline especially in manufacturing industries as robots continue to replace assembly line workers and computers, word processors, and automated office systems carry on replacing some office workers. These changes towards more capital intensive production result in:

  - higher efficiency and increased productivity

  - reduction of hazardous or repetitive tasks

  - use of new techniques or industrial processes

TERMS

Use your own words to distinguish between **labour intensive** and **capital intensive** industries.

_____

_____

APPLICATION

1.   Collect information about a job that could interest you. Try to find out the following information.
   a) What level of education is required?

   _____

   b) How much training or experience is needed?

   _____

   c) What is the starting wage or salary?

   _____

   d) What are the prospects for promotion?

   _____

   e) How easy will it be to get this type of job?

   _____

   f) How secure will the job be?

   _____

2. Compare the information you have just collected for a job that might interest you with the information collected by your classmates for other types of employment.

   a) Which types of jobs are relatively easy to find?

   _____

   b) Which types of jobs are relatively insecure?

   _____

   c) Which jobs require a high level of education?

   _____

   d) Which jobs could involve having to move away to another city?

   _____

3. Suggest a reason for each of the following facts.

   a) A baseball player earns over a million dollars a season.

   _____

   b) A helper at McDonald's earns only the minimum wage per hour.

   _____

   c) A worker with 15 years seniority earns more than a beginner.

   _____

   d) A member of the plumbers' union earns more than an equally competent non-unionized plumber.

   _____

   e) A male manager earns more than a female manager.

   _____

   f) Dishwashers earn about $200 a week while some welders can earn over $2 000 a week.

   _____

   g) Workers at a remote project earn more than workers engaged in similar jobs in the Montréal area.

   _____

   h) Some workers are willing to accept lower wages during a depression.

   _____

   i) A manager with little experience earns more than a production worker with ten years of experience.

   _____

The basic structure of unions

OUTLINE

Despite frequent news reports about labour unions and strikes, in Canada only about one worker in three belongs to a union and most unions reach agreements with the employer without having to resort to a strike. In Québec the public sector is more unionized than the private sector.

Workers in large companies, especially those in the manufacturing sector, tend to be unionized. Unions are not common in the tertiary sector. In fact, there is strong resistance from banks, real estate companies, retail stores, hotels and restaurants to having their workers form a union. Women tend to be less unionized than men because they form a relatively large proportion of the labour force in the tertiary sector.

Reasons for trade unions / labour unions

- to *counter exploitation* of workers by some employers
- to *improve working conditions* of the members
- to *obtain better wages and fringe benefits* (holidays, sick pay, pension schemes, daycare facilities)
- to *protect the buying power and job security* of members

Certification of a union

Before a union can start any type of action on behalf of an employee or a group of employees it has to be **accredited** *(obtain official authorization to form a union)*. It must take the following steps:

1 Some workers try to recruit others. This must be done out of working hours and outside the place of employment. The employer does not have the right to prevent the formation of a union.

2 Those who wish to join the proposed union sign a membership card and pay at least $2 as a membership fee.

3 Once 35% to 50% of the workers have signed a membership card, the organizers can ask the government for **accreditation**. If more than 50% of the workers vote for the union, it is recognized by the Ministère du Travail and it becomes officially accredited or certified.

4 Once certified, the union has to negotiate a **collective agreement** with the employer. The employer is not allowed to refuse employment or fire a worker for being a member or director of a union.

5 The employer has to collect union dues from all workers benefitting from the collective agreement. The dues are deducted from each pay cheque according to a law known as the **Rand formula**.

Types of unions

1 **Craft unions** organize workers according to particular skills or occupations: e.g. *United Brotherhood of Carpenters*.

2 **Industrial unions** organize workers in a particular industry irrespective of their skill or occupation: e.g. *United Automobile Workers of Canada, Canadian Union of Public Employees*.

3 **General unions** organize workers regardless of skill or industry: e.g. *Teamsters Union*.

4 **Company unions** are those which have been organized largely by the employer.

- **Open shops** exist where workers are free to join the union or not. All benefit from the collective agreement.

- **Closed shops** exist where workers must belong to the union to be able to work at a particular location.

Levels of organization

- The basic level is the place of work: the plant, the office, or the business establishment. This unit is called a **local**. It is responsible for the negotiation and application of the collective agreement.

- Most unions are affiliated with national *(Canada)* or international unions *(United States and Canada)*. These large unions combine the interests and strengths of the locals. They back the locals with financial assistance, strike funds, lawyers, research facilities, expertise in negotiations, and they may coordinate boycotts and strike action.

- Most national or international unions are affiliated with the national congress or federation. The congress acts as a pressure group in matters of general interest to workers, especially in promoting legislation favourable to workers.

- In Canada the congress is called the *Canadian Labour Congress* (CLC). In the United States it is the *American Federation of Labour and Congress of Industrial Organizations* (AFL / CIO).

- In Québec most unions belong to a ***centrale*** such as the CNTU or the CSQ. *(See next section.)*

APPLICATION

1. Label the diagram to illustrate the relationship between locals, unions, and a federation of unions.

2. Find out which workers in your area are unionized and which are not. List their companies or types of job in the columns below.

UNIONIZED WORKERS	NON-UNIONIZED WORKERS

3. Collect articles about current or recent strikes. What are the issues?

_____

_____

_____

_____

_____

_____

_____

4. Why do you think some sectors such as employees of banks, gasoline stations, and fast-food outlets are hard to unionize?

_____

_____

_____

_____

_____

_____

_____

_____

The role of trade unions

OUTLINE

Unions are created to protect the social and economic interests of their members and to improve their working conditions. To achieve these goals unions are organized in different ways. In Québec there are both vertical and horizontal patterns of organization.

Vertical organization

- Workers are organized in small units called **locals**. They share common problems and it is usually possible for all to meet and participate in discussions about contracts and labour disputes.
- Within the same occupation or industry there are other locals which experience very similar problems and needs. Thus, it is advantageous for all their locals to belong to a **union** which has enough funds to hire a permanent staff to look after the collective needs of the members and provide specialized advice and legal aid to locals. The union coordinates the actions of the locals.
- Each local has its own certificate and voting rights. Its members have the right to vote on important issues such as union dues, whether to strike, election of union officers, and changes to the constitution.
- The locals have to be consulted by the union executive before it makes any major moves.

Horizontal organization

- Because several unions have similar problems such as negotiating with the government in the public sector or adapting to changing technology in the private sector, it is sometimes advantageous to create horizontal ties.
- In Québec such organizations are called **centrales** or **federations**. In English Canada many unions belong to the *Canadian Federation of Labour* (CFL). International unions belong to the AFL/CIO.
- The term **centrale** refers to a federation of autonomous unions. As a large body representing many thousands of workers, a centrale can deal more effectively with governments and powerful employer groups.
- In Québec there are four centrales which are usually known by their acronyms *(the initials of the main words in their name)*:

  1 **QFL** *(Québec Federation of Labour)* / **FTQ** *(Fédération des travailleurs du Québec)*

  This is the biggest centrale. It groups unions which operate mainly in the private sector. It tends to be less nationalistic in its orientations.

  2 **CNTU** *(Confederation of National Trade Unions)* / **CSN** *(Confédération des syndicats nationaux)*

  This centrale developed from a group of unions with strong ties to the Roman Catholic Church. Since the 1960s the CNTU has turned away from its early religious orientation towards a concern for social justice and the quality of life. It tends to represent unions with workers in poorly paid occupations. The hospital and social affairs workers mostly belong to this centrale.

  3 **CSQ** *(Centrale syndicale du Québec)* formerly **CEQ** *(Centrale de l'enseignement du Québec)*

  This centrale ties together about 100 000 workers in the education sector as well as some 40 000 members from other sectors of public employment such as nurses, day-care workers, recreation, and communications. The new name reflects this diversity.

  4 **CSD** *(Centrale des syndicats démocratiques)*

  This is the smallest centrale with members mostly in the industrial sector. It broke away from the CNTU in 1972 mainly because of ideological differences. Its growth has been slow.

- There are also independent trade unions which do not belong to any centrale.
- For negotiations involving new contracts in the public sector the centrales sometimes form a **common front**. The leaders and executives of the three largest centrales attempt to harmonize their demands and their strategies to present a united common front to the government and the employer groups. It can be a powerful pressure tactic, but it is hard to arrange.

APPLICATION

1. Talk with your teachers and the support staff in your school to find out about the structure of the labour organization to which they belong.

    a) Does it seem democratically operated to you?

    _____

    _____

    b) Do the leaders of the centrales seem to truly represent the views of ordinary "grass roots" members?

    _____

    _____

2. Are labour unions a good thing for the workers, or do you feel they have too much power?

    Discuss this question with some friends or with your family. Record you conclusions below.

    _____

    _____

    _____

    _____

    _____

    _____

    _____

    _____

    _____

    _____

    _____

BAC AIC BCC D CD A BIC B BIC BAB cc DD
1 2 3   4   5 6 7   8 9   10   11   12   13   14 15 16 17 18 19 20

Labour contracts: - negotiation procedures

OUTLINE

Collective bargaining refers to the procedures by which a group of workers *(a union or syndicate)* negotiates remuneration and fringe benefits with their employer. This use of collective strength to negotiate with an employer is beneficial to most workers because otherwise each employee would be forced to negotiate his/her working conditions individually with the employer. Only in rare cases would an individual be of comparable strength to the employer. Any complaints by individuals concerning working conditions could be solved easily by replacing the worker. Collective bargaining protects individuals from reprisals by the employer.

Collective bargaining procedures

(The exact procedure followed varies according to circumstances for each negotiation. Each possible action is described below in the approximate order in which it would occur.)

- The members of the union decide on their collective **demand** for changes in pay, working conditions, and fringe benefits. The members vote and the executive is given a mandate to obtain as much of the demand as possible.

- The employer organization decides what it is prepared to give, if anything. This is the employer's **offer**.

- After the demand and the offer have been presented, the two parties begin **negotiations**. In <u>most cases</u> meaningful negotiations result in a new collective agreement signed by the two sides. The new **collective agreement** or **contract** is binding for both parties usually for one to three years.

However, <u>if the employer(s) and the union(s) cannot agree</u>, further steps are taken.

- If negotiations break down it is possible to ask the Minister of Labour to appoint a **conciliator** or a **mediator** to try to help resolve the differences. A conciliator makes suggestions. A mediator proposes a contract. Mediators are government employees and both sides must participate with them. Their recommendations are not binding and can be rejected. Both the conciliator and the mediator have to send a report to the minister.

- If negotiations are proving fruitless, either side may decide to resort to **pressure tactics**. If a majority of the members present have approved in a secret vote, the union can call a **strike** *(the workers refuse to work and then set up picket lines to enforce the ban)*. They can also decide to **work-to-rule** or engage in a **slowdown** or practise **rotating strikes** to put pressure on the employer to negotiate more seriously. During a strike, management may keep the business in operation by doing the workers' tasks itself, but the law forbids the use of **scabs** *(non-union replacement workers brought in to break the strike)*. The employer may declare a **lockout** and close down the factory to put pressure on the workers.

- A strike or a lockout can result in some unpleasant situations, even violence. Should it appear that no solution will be forthcoming there remains the possibility of **arbitration**. The request for arbitration must come from both sides. Three arbitrators are selected and they consider both sides of the dispute in great depth. The decisions of the arbitrators are legally binding on both sides so this is not a popular method of solving disputes.

- In the case of a strike which is harmful to the public interest, the government may decide to pass a special law or **decree** which forces the workers to return to work and sets out the conditions of employment. Often the threat of a special law is sufficient to persuade the sides to reach a compromise agreement.

- Sometimes the company decides to **close** its plant rather than make an unacceptable deal with its workers. This is more likely when the plant is inefficient or outdated. Small plants that are part of a multinational or a large company can be closed without much effect on the total operations of the company.

- During the life of a collective agreement the union and management do not always agree on the **interpretation** of certain clauses. The union or the management can file a **grievance**. If the two sides cannot settle the matter themselves, the case is taken to an *arbitration court* for a decision which is legally binding.

Court injunctions

Sometimes one of the two sides in a contract dispute will make an appeal to the judicial system to make a decision in its favour. The issue is taken to court and a judge is asked for an **injunction** *(an order by the court to the other party in the action to desist from some activity which is causing a problem)* which is usually granted for a limited period while contract negotiations continue, but an injunction can be permanent. Injunctions are mostly requested by employers who believe public safety or interests are being endangered, but unions may also ask for an injunction; for example, to have a lockout lifted.

APPLICATION

1. The diagram presents a simplified outline of possible methods used to obtain a collective agreement. The labels listed below have been omitted from the diagram. Place each label in the most appropriate box on the diagram.

LABELS TO BE INSERTED

ARBITRATION   LOCKOUT
CLOSURE OF PLANT   MEDIATION
CONCILIATION   UNION'S DEMAND
EMPLOYER'S OFFER

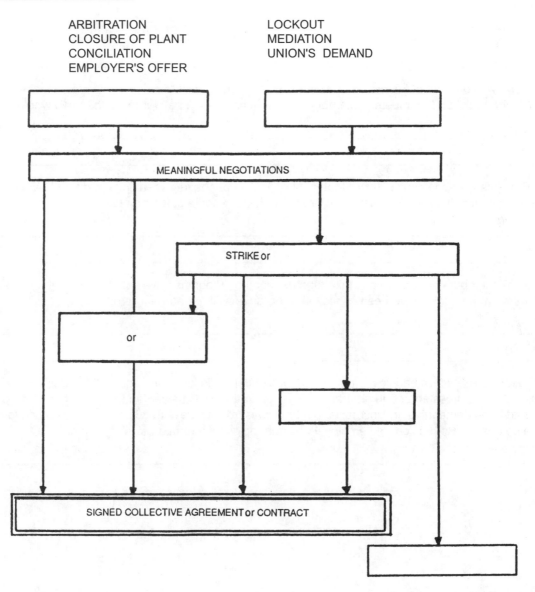

67

2. Consider each of the following cases and use your knowledge of labour-management negotiating procedures to suggest *what should or may happen next*.

a) The current three year contract between Local 257 of the United Widget Workers Union (UWWU) and the Bloggins Gadget Company will expire in three months time.

_____

_____

b) Bloggins has been very successful for the last three years and has lots of orders on the books. There have been very few grievances about the current contract which will soon expire.

_____

_____

c) The company has made very little profit this year and has few new orders. Management is not satisfied with productivity. The workers want a 15% wage increase to give them parity with workers in similar factories in Ontario.

_____

_____

d) After three weeks of tough bargaining the two sides seem to be getting nowhere, but neither party wants to break off the discussions.

_____

_____

e) Local 257 would like to put some pressure on Bloggins, but UWWU's strike funds are almost exhausted and most of the Local 257 members could not manage without strike pay for more than two weeks.

_____

_____

f) The Bloggins' management is aware that most of its workers have few savings and that UWWU is unable to give them much strike pay so it wants to pressure them to settle quickly on its terms.

_____

_____

g) Local 257 members have been on strike for nine months. Bloggins have sold their inventory of gadgets and all orders on the books have been cancelled. The union will not agree to arbitration.

_____

_____

h) After a long strike which had cost Bloggins millions of dollars in lost sales and had used up the UWWU strike funds, the two parties agreed to arbitration. The arbitration board awarded the workers much less pay than they had been demanding and increased paid holidays from 10 days to 30 days a year - much to the disgust of the company. Both union and employer are unhappy with the arbitrators' decisions.

_____

_____

Labour contracts: - collective agreements

OUTLINE

A **collective agreement** establishes the rules which the employer and employees must follow in their working relationship. These rules relate to salary matters, fringe benefits, and working conditions.

Monetary clauses

- Some of the clauses in the collective agreement have a dollar value. These are monetary clauses.
- Detailed **wage scales** are included for each category of worker. They show starting wages and the increment *(increase)* attached to each step in the scale. Usually the scales are advanced upwards by an agreed on percentage for each year of the contract.
- Sometimes there is a **cost of living** clause. If the annual inflation rate rises above a certain percentage, the scales will be adjusted automatically upwards without new negotiations. This is also called **indexation of salaries**.
- The number of hours in a regular work week are stipulated. **Overtime rates** are stated, if applicable.
- Detailed job descriptions are often included in this section to avoid arguments about the satisfactory / unsatisfactory performance of individual workers and the reasonable / unreasonable expectations of some managers.
- **Monetary fringe benefits** are included because they also cost money. The most common are:
  - the number of paid **holidays**
  - **absences with pay** for matters such as maternity leave, illness, disability, death in the family, marriage, further training
  - **pension** contributions to government schemes and to the company plan too in many instances
  - **insurance** payments for health, life, and long-term disability. Usually the employer pays a part of the contribution to health insurance.

Working conditions

- **Safety regulations** are clearly set out especially if part of the process is hazardous or dangerous to the health of the workers.
- Rules for establishing **seniority** *(the comparable length of time a worker has been with the company)* are set out because this affects certain promotions or the order in which workers can be laid off. It attempts to avoid accusations of favouritism on the part of the employer.
- Criteria for **promotion** or for **incompetence** *(unsatisfactory work performance)* are stated.
- Procedures for settling **grievances** are outlined.
- The **length** of the contract is stated.
- Collection of **union dues** according to the Rand formula is noted.
- More and more companies are now including an **employee assistance** clause which offers help to employees facing problems related to finances, marriage, alcohol, or drugs.

Grievances

- Most collective agreements are long documents written in dry legal terms, but for the most part they work. Like any legal document, the contract is open to misinterpretation and/or misapplication. When problems develop it is possible for either the employer or the union to file a grievance with a special labour court to determine the "correct" interpretation. The judge (or often the tribunal) hears evidence from both sides of the case and then passes judgment. This grievance procedure is important because it is the only way to ensure that a collective agreement will be applied.

APPLICATION

1. Explain why it is important to include the following sections in a collective agreement.

    a) Clauses about seniority

    _____

    _____

    b) Detailed pay scales for each category of employment

    _____

    _____

    c) Details about paid holidays and leave of absence with pay

    _____

    _____

    d) Detailed job descriptions

    _____

    _____

    e) Regulations about health and safety in the work place

    _____

    _____

2. Collective bargaining refers to the ability of any group of workers to negotiate its working conditions. Should some groups of workers be exempt from this choice? Should they have their wages and working conditions imposed on them, or do they have the right to negotiate and, if necessary, strike to force negotiations?

    Summarize your views on this issue below.

    _____

    _____

    _____

    _____

    _____

    _____

    _____

    _____

    _____

    _____

    _____

The role of the State

Governments play a large role in the mixed economic system of Canada and Québec. With respect to labour, governments pass regulations and laws covering relationships between employers and employees, but they are also the direct employers of many civil servants and the indirect employers of parapublic sector workers such as teachers and hospital workers.

The Labour Codes

- As Canada became industrialized the need for laws covering working conditions became evident. The federal government passes laws for services such as banking, railways, airlines, and the post office which operate on a country-wide basis. About 90% of workers fall under provincial jurisdiction.

- By now, so many laws and regulations have been passed that they have been grouped together or "codified" into the **Labour Code**.

- **The Canada Labour Code** prohibits job discrimination. This has been reinforced by the creation of the Canadian Human Rights Commission. The code limits the length of the working day (8 hours) and the working week. It also guarantees minimum wages and stipulates overtime provisions, describes procedure for layoffs (including length of notice and severance payments) and maternity leaves as well as describing job safety and strike procedures. The *Employment Insurance Act* is also a federal government initiative.

- **The Quebec Labour Code**
    - contains similar regulations for workers who fall under provincial jurisdiction
    - describes the process of union certification
    - sets the minimum and maximum periods of a collective agreement
    - makes secret ballots mandatory for the election of union officers, seeking a strike mandate, or ratifying a collective agreement
    - prohibits management from hiring scabs during the period of a legal strike
    - sets up mechanisms for arbitration procedures
    - grants the right to strike to most workers in the public and parapublic sectors
    - The ***Act Regulating Labour Standards*** sets out the basic rights of workers e.g. minimum wages, the standard workweek, statutory holidays, annual leave, leaves for family events. It applies to all workers but it is the only legal protection for non-unionized workers who do not have a collective agreement.
    - Other important Quebec laws are the *Minimum Wage Act*, the *Occupational Health and Safety Act*, and the *Industrial Accidents and Occupational Diseases Act*.

The State as an employer

- Different levels of government employ about one third of Canadian workers in one capacity or another: e.g. civil servants, armed forces, teachers, police, municipal workers, hospital workers, employees of crown corporations.
- Civil servants and armed forces personnel are paid directly by the government. Parapublic employees are paid by a school board or hospital which is funded by the government. Crown corporations pay their workers from their operating budget.
- Traditionally, salaries paid in the public sector averaged less than those paid for equivalent work in the private sector. In the past, this was considered acceptable by many because of the much greater job security of public sector workers. In addition, for many years public employees did not have the right to strike or even form a union in some cases.
- Today, the public sector is highly unionized and most workers enjoy the right to strike. When there is a strike in the public sector the government is placed in a delicate situation; it is both the employer and the arbitrator if the issues cannot be resolved through negotiations. In labour disputes involving unions and employers in the private sector the state can attempt to intervene as an unbiased third party. In public sector negotiations it is part of the employer group as well as being the final arbitrator of disputes.
- Much depends on the political philosophy of the ruling party. Social democratic governments tend to favour the workers at the expense of the owners. Conservative, right-wing parties tend to favour free-enterprise and the employers. In times of recession they may even roll back wages and salaries already agreed to in contracts.
- If negotiations seem deadlocked, the government can pass a **decree** forcing its employees back to work on its own terms.

APPLICATION

1. Determine the attitudes towards labour of the present governments of:

   a) Canada _____

   b) Québec _____

   c) Ontario _____

   d) British Columbia _____

   e) United States _____

   f) United Kingdom _____

2. Find out which public sector workers currently have their salaries and working conditions set by:

   a) a collective agreement signed by their union and the government's negotiators

   _____

   _____

   b) a decree passed by the government which employs them

   _____

   _____

3. Try to discover the current standards for the following in Québec.

   a) Minimum wage (General rate) _____ (For employees who receive tips) _____

   b) Standard workweek (General) _____ (For domestics residing with the employer) _____

   c) Annual leave (1 to 10 years) _____ Employed 10 years and over _____

   d) Maternity leave (before birth) _____ Parental leave (after birth / adoption) _____

   e) Marriage (of employee) _____ Funeral of close relative _____

4. Disputes between the government and workers in the public sector gain much publicity because they often involve essential services on which many people depend. They may even result in hardship for some citizens.

   Should strikes be permitted in hospitals or the postal service or in public transportation or in schools? What are your feelings on this issue?

   _____

   _____

   _____

   _____

   _____

   _____

Module 4

CONSUMPTION

OBJECTIVES

4.1 *Analyze the phenomenon of consumption.*

4.2 *Establish the link between credit and rational consumption.*

4.3 *Use different means of consumer protection.*

4.4 *Describe and explain different ways of using surplus income to advantage.*

We are all consumers and most of us would consume more goods and services if we could afford them. What are the factors that influence our buying habits? To what extent are we influenced by advertising? How can consumers use credit to make purchases? How can the consumer use credit with caution to avoid getting into debt beyond his ability to repay? What rights do consumers have and what are their responsibilities? How can consumers be protected? What laws and agencies exist to promote fair practices in the market place? These important questions will be addressed in this module.

In addition, it will consider reasons for saving a part of our disposable income and help us make decisions about the best ways to invest our savings so that they earn a reasonable income.

Factors of consumption

OUTLINE

Consumption refers to the use of goods and services to satisfy present needs and wants. **Consumers** are the people, the companies, and the public institutions which buy the goods and services.

Today we live in a **consumer society** in which we are urged to buy many goods and services that are not absolutely necessary and which will not be used for long. If we did not engage in **mass consumption** then there would be less demand for all the goods made by **mass production** methods in our factories.

Factors affecting consumption

- **needs and wants**
    - Vital needs such as food, clothing, and shelter usually take priority.
    - Wants vary from person to person.
    - Personal needs and wants are a matter of individual choice.
    - Collective needs of society are dealt with by governments and public institutions.

- **disposable income** *(income that remains after all deductions at source have been made)*
    - For many it is their **net pay**; for others it is employment insurance or health insurance payments; for a few it derives from investment sources or inheritance.
    - When disposable income is low most money has to be spent on basic needs.
    - When disposable income is high there is more money to spend on wants or to save. Savings can be considered as **deferred consumption**.
    - Disposable income can be temporarily increased by obtaining **credit** *("buy now, pay later")* However, people with low incomes may find it difficult to obtain credit. People tend to use credit less when interest rates are high.
    - **Inflation** tends to reduce the amount of disposable income that can be spent on wants. Thus, in periods of inflation there is pressure to increase wages, salaries, pensions, and allowances.

- **level of education**
    - People with more knowledge about consumer matters tend to make wiser consumer decisions.
    - More educated people tend to have more disposable income so they buy more and often choose goods in higher price ranges.

- **age**
    - Our needs and our tastes change with age:
    - Young children have very simple needs, parents make choices for them.
    - Teenagers have more varied needs and wants; much affected by current fashions and fads; easily influenced by peers; disposable income is relatively low.
    - Young adults spend more on cars, clothes, travel, sports activities, and leisure.
    - Families with young children spend more on houses, furniture, children's needs, insurance.
    - Older people have fewer consumer needs but spend more on health care.

- **price**
    - We often consider the relative prices of goods. The **relative price** is the price of one good or service compared to the price of other goods and services. If the latest fashion costs 5 times more than the "store brand" price for a similar item, we may decide to buy the cheaper product.
    - If the price falls low enough we are tempted to buy a "bargain" or to purchase more than we need to "stock up".
    - When the price is high we are more likely to consider the **opportunity cost** of the good or service *(what we have to do without if we spend our money on that good or service)*.
    - Sometimes we are willing to pay higher prices to obtain better quality.

- **lifestyle**
  - Young people are used to our modern "leisure society" which has more time to spend on leisure activities. Spend more on fast foods, entertainment, clothes, sports, travel.
  - Identifiable groups such as "yuppies" and "bikers" consume according to the style of the group.

- **culture**
  - Many consumer habits are learned from our parents or the society in which we live.
  - Attitudes to buying on credit, choosing quality, satisfying wants, etc. depend on <u>where</u> and <u>when</u> a person is brought up.

TERMS

Explain these terms in your own words:

consumption _is when people use things or services to feel immediately satisfied_

disposable income _Spending power a person has_

relative price _the price of one item or service compared to a similar other item or service_

APPLICATION

1   Give at least three examples of each of the following:

a) vital needs _food, clothing, shelter_

b) less essential needs _fashionable clothing, higher education, haircut_

c) some wants that you have satisfied recently

travelling, snacks, concert

d) the **opportunity cost** of satisfying the wants that you chose

sell something else, get a higher paying job, ask for a loan

2   Identify the main factor(s) affecting each of the following consumer choices.

a) A man with six grandchildren buys a hearing aid. _less essential need_

b) A family on welfare switches from steak to hamburger. _lack of disposable income / need_

c) A Jewish family purchases kosher foods. _less essential need_

d) A young successful lawyer buys a Porsche sports car. _level of education / age / want_

e) A woman living on an Old Age Security allowance decides to rent a smaller apartment. _age / relative price_

3   Consider each of the following cases while completing the chart below. What factors are likely to influence the choices made about consumption in each case? *Suggest the approximate percentage of income that will be spent in each category.*

CASE A   Girl aged 17 from middle-class family. Receives $50.00 allowance per week.

CASE B   Boy aged 12 from single-parent home. Income of $30.00 a week from paper route.

CASE C   Couple with three children aged 2, 4, and 7. Total income of $350.00 a week.

CASE D   Ambitious professional couple aged 28 and 30. Combined income of $1 550.00 a week.

	CASE A %	CASE B %	CASE C %	CASE D %
FIXED EXPENSES Rent/mortgage	X	X	30%	10%
Heat, electricity	X	X	4%	1%
Telephone	X	X	2%	1%
Insurance	X	X	5%	3%
Taxes	X	X	X	X
Payments on loans	X	X	10%	5%
VARIABLE EXPENSES Transportation	X	10%	10%	8%
Food for home	X	20%	15%	10%
Restaurants	15%	20%	X	8%
Clothing	30%	X	10%	8%
Household goods	X		9%	4%
Entertainment	30%	20%	X	10%
Beverages	15%	10%	3%	5%
Tobacco	X	X	X	4%
Personal care	10%	X	5%	4%
Education	X	X	X	X
Savings	X	10%	X	20%

4   Imagine you are 21 years old and your wants include a college education, a sports car, your own apartment, and a holiday in Florida. What factor(s) would affect your decisions about consumption if:
a)   your disposable income is $25 000 a year?

   lifestyle, disposable income

b)   your income is $8 000 but both your parents are unemployed?

   culture, relative price, credit

c)   your income is $10 000 but there is rapid inflation?

   disposable income, relative price, credit

The importance of advertising

OUTLINE

Advertising is a message designed to persuade people to buy one product instead of another. Producers use visual and spoken ads to convince consumers. The aim is to attract, interest, inform consumers. The intent is to persuade them to buy the product.

- **impact on production**
  - Advertising increases demand for a product which in turn increases production.
  - Cuts costs and raises profits

- **impact on consumption**
  Directed at the intellectual, emotional, and subconscious levels of consumers:
  - Appeals to our *intelligence* by giving more factual information.
  - Appeals to our *emotions* by playing on fears, desire to be liked, etc.
  - Appeal is *subconscious* when it associates a lifestyle with a product. Sometimes this appeal is *subliminal (we are unaware that it is appealing to our subconscious)*
  - Used to introduce new products.
  - Tries to convince consumers to switch from one brand to another.
  - "Loss leaders" attract consumers to the store in the hope they will buy other goods at regular prices.
  - Announces "sales" to persuade people to go shopping
  - Circulars are used to aim advertising at a given area.
  - Free magazines advertise expensive items in districts where average income is high.
  - Some advertisements are aimed at a particular group.

- **advertising techniques**
  - *Repetition* - say it often enough and they believe it
  - *Scare techniques* - bad breath, body odors, plaque
  - *Snob appeal* - keep up with high trends or the "cool" set
  - *Imitation* -"get on board" - enjoy the product and have a good time like everyone else
  - *Association* with a celebrity who endorses the product
  - *Comfort and enjoyment* - suggesting we will enjoy more success if we use the product
  - *Humour* - makes you laugh to get your attention

- **objective and subjective advertising**
  - *Objective advertising* informs, appeals to the intellect. Gives details about the dealer, product, size, price, and benefits/ harmful effects. Helps consumer to practise **comparison shopping** and save money or find the most suitable product.
  - *Subjective advertising* concentrates on selling a product, appeals to emotions and subconscious. Tends to stress social benefits and lifestyles. Sometimes a well-known person tells how satisfied he/she is with the product, suggesting you will be like that person if you use the product.

- **problems related to advertising**
  - Misleading ads which do not tell all.
  - Create unreasonable expectations. Promote unnecessary consumption, strain budgets, even cause depression in a few people.
  - Costs of advertising are included in the cost of the product. (However, increased sales can result in lower prices if the reduction in costs is passed on to the consumer.)

TERMS

Explain these terms in your own words:

advertising _a visual or an audio presentation of an idea that a product or service will enhance your life_

comparison shopping _finding what one feels to be the best balance of quality, quantity & price of a product or service._

APPLICATION

1   Which type(s) of advertising is/are represented by each of the following examples?

a)   A soft drink commercial showing young people having fun.   _Imitation_

b)   A medical association warning about the harmful effects of smoking.   _Scare technique_

c)   "Pants 50% off!" (*but the original price is not mentioned*)   _Sales_

d)   "How you can lose weight . . .naturally and deliciously . . . in two weeks"   _Comfort & enjoyment_

e)   "CLEARANCE – up to 70% off regular prices"   _Sales_

f)   A photo of a muscular "hunk" on an advertisement for a health clinic   _Snob appeal_

g)   A photo of a starving child on a circular for a charitable appeal   _Scare technique, appeal to emotions_

2   How do different advertising techniques affect you? Which appeal to you the most? Complete the table below to discover your preferences.

ADVERTISING TECHNIQUE	EFFECTS ON YOU		
	Strong appeal	Some appeal	Little appeal
Repetition			✓
Humour	✓		
Snob appeal		✓	
Scare			✓
Conformity			✓
Imitation		✓	
Enjoyment	✓		

3   Try to recall some of the television commercials you have seen in the last few days. Select the one which you find:

   a) most effective and appealing   _____

   b) most offensive and annoying   _____any Brand Power commercial_____

   c) Compare your choices with those of others. Have a discussion and try to agree on a winner in each category.

4   Find examples of different types of advertising in discarded newspapers or magazines. Paste some of them in the space below if they are small enough. If not, write a brief description of the content of the advertisement. Decide which advertising technique is being used for each example you give.

Consumer credit

OUTLINE

Credit allows the consumer <u>immediate use</u> of goods, services, or money in return for a promise to pay back later *with interest*. It involves:

- enjoying immediate use of goods and/or services
- using a financial institution's money for a period of time
- paying interest charges for a period of time
- paying back the original amount over the duration of the loan

It is useful to distinguish between **business credit** which is used to help companies and governments finance the costs of materials, expansion projects, and operating costs and **consumer credit** which is used by individuals to "buy now and pay later" for goods, services, and real estate that they would like to enjoy now.

Advantages of credit buying

- Buying on credit is *convenient* -Consumers can take advantage of sales; there is no need to carry large sums of cash.
- It *increases the purchasing power* of the consumer; there is no need to wait till cash is available. It establishes a **credit rating** *(an evaluation of a person's credit-worthiness based on income and previous`record for repaying debts)* with a local Credit Bureau.
- The *merchant sells more*, makes an immediate sale.
- It helps to *even out consumer demand* which results in stability of employment.
- It raises the general standard of living.

Disadvantages of credit buying

- It may give a *false perception* of real purchasing power and result in the consumer living beyond his/her means.
- The consumer may become a victim of *impulse buying* which can lead to overspending.
- It is easy to accumulate *too much debt* and possibly build up insolvable debt.
- There is a possibility of *credit card fraud* if the card is lost or stolen or if the number of the card is known to others.

The cost of credit

Before signing any retail credit contract the consumer should know:

- exactly *what is being purchased* - a clear description on the document is required
- the *cash price* of the article - or the principal amount in the case of a loan
- the amount of the *down payment* (if any)
- the *rate of interest* as an annual percentage - and is it fixed or variable *(can be changed)*
- the total amount of the *credit charges* over the life of the loan expressed in dollars
- the amount of any *insurance or service charges*
- the *total amount of debt* to be paid
- the *amount, frequency, and due dates of payments*
- the *penalties for defaults* on payments

Determining the consumer's credit-worthiness

Before granting credit the lender will check the consumer's ability to repay the loan. This may involve contacting the local Credit Bureau. Factors usually taken into account are:

- general *character* of the customer - age, honesty, good credit rating in the past. Some may ask for **character references**
- *capacity to repay* - total income, job security, current financial situation including debts
- **collateral** - *property* or other *financial resources* that can be claimed if the loan is not repaid. Some may ask for **guarantors** or **endorsers** who will accept responsibility for repayment in case of default
- *economic conditions in general* - Strikes, layoffs, and recessions make it harder to obtain credit

TERMS

Explain these terms in your own words

consumer credit _being lent small amounts of money to be paid back with interest so one can have use something immediately._

credit rating _a number stating how trustworthy you are to lend money to_

guarantor _someone who agrees to pay off another's debt if they default._

APPLICATION

1. Think of the ways in which most families use credit. Briefly describe four examples of ways in which buying on credit is a convenience for the consumer.

    a) _House_

    b) _groceries_

    c) _Car_

    d) _vacation._

2. When you are applying for credit, why is it reasonable for the lender to ask for details about:

    a) your age, your occupation, where you live?

    to assess your credit worthiness and financial stability

    b) your salary and your current debts to other lenders?

    to know if you are more likely to pay them back.

    c) how long you have lived in the district, how long have you held your present job, how secure is it?

    to know if you are stable in your current situation or likely to leave with their money.

    d) what assets do you have?

    to know what they could repossess as collateral if you don't pay back the loan

PERCENTAGE REPORTING SELECTED DEBTS

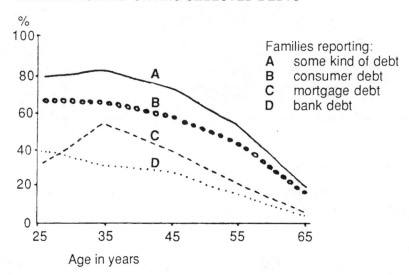

Families reporting:
A   some kind of debt
B   consumer debt
C   mortgage debt
D   bank debt

Age in years

3.   Study the graph and then give reasons why:

a)   the 25 to 45 age group has the largest amount of debt

_____

_____

_____

_____

b)   the over 55 age group has relatively little debt

_____

_____

4.   Aldo would like to buy a new sub-compact car which costs $17 500. He can make a down payment of $3 500. He can obtain a loan for $14 000 at 4% interest. His payments would be $260 per month for 60 months or $420 per month for 36 months.

a)   Calculate the total cost of loans for 60 months and for 36 months. Which is the most advantageous for Aldo?

_____

b)   In your opinion, is it worth it? Give a reason.

_____

_____

_____

_____

Types of consumer credit

There are four main types of consumer credit loans:
- variable credit
- installment plans
- personal loans
- mortgage loans

Variable credit
- **Bank cards** are multipurpose *credit cards* issued by financial institutions such as banks, trust companies, and caisses populaires *(e.g. Visa, MasterCard)*.
  Retail cards are issued by major retail stores, oil companies *(e.g. Canadian Tire, The Bay)*.
  Charge cards are issued by travel and entertainment businesses *(e.g. American Express)*.
- Some are single-use cards *(are honoured only by issuing company)* e.g. Canadian Tire, The Bay, Petro-Canada, Holiday Inn.
- Some are multipurpose cards *(can be used in many retail outlets)* e.g. Visa, MasterCard.
- Bank cards and charge cards have a pre-determined **credit limit** set by the issuer.
- The issuing company sends a monthly statement. If the amount due is paid in full within a stated number of days there is no interest charge.
- If the full amount is not paid by the due date then fairly high interest rates are charged.
- Interest rates are variable *(the bank or company may change them from time to time)*.
- The amount of the loan and repayment period are also flexible. The customer can pay the minimum amount, the full amount due, or an amount in between the two when making a monthly payment.
- The loan is guaranteed by the income, financial standing, and goods of the borrower.
- In case of default, the lender can take legal steps to seize salary and/or belongings of the borrower.

Installment plans
- The consumer signs a **conditional sales contract** which allows him/her to take immediate possession of the good or service, but the seller retains ownership until the final payment is made.
- It involves a **down payment** with subsequent fixed payments at intervals (usually monthly).
- The monthly payment includes interest and service charges.
- These loans are available in many retail stores and travel agencies.
- The interest rate and the repayment period are fixed by the contract.
- If the consumer defaults on payments, the article sold is the guarantee. (The seller may send a legal warning and then, after 30 days, repossess the article if less than half the total amount has been paid. If more than half has been paid, the seller has to obtain permission from a court to repossess the good.)

Personal loans
- Personal loans can be obtained from a bank or caisse populaire or trust company at favourable interest rates if the consumer is a good credit risk.
- They can be obtained from a finance company or a "loan shark" at very high interest rates if the consumer is a poor credit risk.
- The financial institution advertises its lowest rates of interest, but not all consumers qualify for the lowest rate.
- **Collateral** *(security which guarantees repayment of the loan)* and/or a **guarantor** *(a person who co-signs to guarantee repayment)* are needed to obtain a personal loan.
- Personal loans take time to arrange so they are mostly used to consolidate all loans at a more favorable rate, to make a major new purchase, or to cover some unforeseen expense.
- They have a fixed rate of interest and a schedule of monthly payments.

Line of credit
- A pre-arranged loan granted by banks to proven good customers with a high income and assets. Credit can be used up to a fixed maximum amount whenever the need arises without further approval from the bank.

Mortgages
A mortgage is a loan obtained to facilitate the purchase of a property. *(See next section for more information.)*

TERMS

Explain these terms in your own words:

down payment large sum payed at the initial purchase of an item covering part of the cost

collateral assets that can be repossessed if a loan is not paid back

APPLICATION

1. Which type of consumer credit would be most suited for each of the following situations?

   a) The Bensons are successful young professionals with steady jobs and good salaries. They want to purchase a new sports car which costs $28 000.

   loan

   b) John takes Lisa out to dinner in a classy restaurant. The bill is $183 and he does not have enough cash to pay it.

   credit card

   c) Liam and Minh are recent immigrants who have found jobs and are setting up their first apartment. They want to purchase a new refrigerator in a retail store.

   conditional sales contract

   d) Jim Cassidy is a travelling salesman. He needs to fill his car with gasoline at least once a day.

   retail card

   e) Tim and Laura decide to redesign their living room - new carpet, new furniture, new drapes, new accessories, and new paint. They have $5 000 saved to pay for the changes. They want to visit stores and purchase the goods they choose during their summer vacation which lasts only two weeks.

   credit card

2. Credit cards prove to be a great convenience for some consumers and a curse for others.

   a) List the main advantages of credit cards.

   1. -if payed back in time there is no interest
   2. -consumers can spend money that they haven't yet earned
   3. -expensive items can be purchased without large amounts of cash
   4. -raises the general standard of living
   5. -larger quantities can be purchased.

   b) List the principle disadvantages of credit cards.

   1. -high interest rates
   2. -possibility of getting into huge debt
   3. -interest rates are variable
   4. -lender can attempt to seize salary of possessions of consumer

3. Shirley is 18 and she lives at home with her parents. She has steady job which pays about $400 net per week. She has only $500 in her savings account. She wants to buy a second-hand car in reasonable condition but the firm asking price is $5 000.

a) Use these details to complete a loan application form from any lending institution.

b) Pretend you are the loans officer of the lending institution. Would you grant the loan to Shirley?

_____

4 a) Either by looking in the financial section of a newspaper or by making direct inquiries, discover the current interest rates charged by:
- commercial banks
- caisses populaires
- major credit card companies
- finance companies.

b) Rank these sources of consumer credit from the ones with the lowest interest rates to the ones with the highest rates.

LOWEST RATES　　1 _____

　　　　　　　　　2 _____

　　　　　　　　　3 _____

HIGHEST RATES　　4 _____

5. Complete the table below to compare and contrast the main types of consumer credit.

TYPE OF CREDIT	SOURCE(S)	GUARANTEE REQUIRED	ACTION TAKEN IF PAYMENTS NOT MADE
Credit cards	banks trust companies caisses populaires	age, income due date	seize salary or belongings
Installment plans	retail store travel agencies	down payment signing of conditional sales contract	repossession of product purchased on plan
Personal loans	financial institutions	collateral / guarantor	collateral / guarantor pays it off

85

Mortgages

A **mortgage** is a loan obtained to facilitate the purchase of a property *(building and/or land)*. Few people want to wait till they have saved the large amount of capital required to buy a house so they negotiate a mortgage loan. A financial institution is willing to lend a large sum of money for a long period because the mortgage agreement allows it to seize the property and resell it if the borrower defaults on his payments.

A mortgage is a legal agreement between the purchaser (borrower) and the financial institution (lender). It is a legal document drawn up by a **notary** which states the following:
- description and location of the property
- amount of money borrowed
- rate of interest charged
- duration of the loan
- number of payments (monthly, biweekly, or weekly)
- amount per payment - which includes **principal** and interest (and sometimes municipal taxes too)
- insurance coverage requirements - fire insurance is compulsory
- **foreclosure** procedures *(what the financial institution will do if you fail to make payments)*

The property is the collateral for the mortgage. The loan may be up to 95% of the appraised value of some properties for first-time home buyers or those who have not owned a principal residence any time during the last five years. Conventional mortgages are usually in the 70% to 80% range.

Sources of mortgages are trust companies, caisses populaires, credit unions, chartered banks, life insurance companies, and the Canada Housing and Mortgage Corporation (CMHC) provided the borrower meets their criteria.

Types of mortgages
- **Open mortgages** - Principal can be repaid at any time without penalty so the interest rate is slightly higher.

- **Closed mortgages** - Principal may be paid off only at specific times of year usually at the "anniversary" date. A penalty is enforced if the principal is paid off sooner.

- **Variable rate mortgages** -The financial institution determines the rate of interest each month so the fixed monthly payments may do little to reduce the principal if interest rates rise.

- **Existing mortgages** - An already existing mortgage is transferred to the new owner of the property. This is very attractive if the mortgage loan was obtained when interest rates were lower.

In the early years of a mortgage a very high proportion of the fixed monthly payment goes to cover interest payments and not to reduce principal. Because the amount borrowed is normally considerable, mortgage payments are usually spread over a long period (15 to 25 years). When rates are changeable many prefer to renegotiate after a period of 1 to 5 years. The total amount paid in interest over the period of a long mortgage greatly exceeds the amount of the original loan. (Often double or more!)

Buying versus renting a house
- Buying means losing the interest on the down payment for the house and the opportunity cost. Regular mortgage payments, taxes, utilities, heating, and repair represent considerable costs, but the value tends to increase over a long period and acts as a hedge against inflation so it can prove a good investment. For many, owning a house fulfils a dream and provides a stable location.
- Renting means having money to invest or spend on other goods and services. Rents tend to rise each year and there is nothing to show for rent payments. The tenant has no ownership title and no investment in the dwelling. It is easy to move to a new location so flexible for those who may need to transfer.

TERMS

Explain these terms in your own words:

mortgage _____

_____

foreclosure _____

_____

APPLICATION

1. Interpret the diagram which shows the relationship between interest charges and principal repayments during the course of a mortgage.

   Mortgage payments: principal and interest

   a) Describe the relationship near the beginning of the mortgage.

   _____

   b) Describe the relationship near the end of the mortgage.

   _____

   INTEREST

   PRINCIPAL

   0   10   20

   Amortization period in years

2. Study the table showing data relative to a $100 000 mortgage.

$100 000 mortgage

	20 year amortization			25 year amortization		
Interest rate	Monthly payment	Total repaid	Total interest payments	Monthly payment	Total repaid	Total interest payments
7%	$769	$184 634	$84 634	$700	$210 123	$110 123
8%	$828	$198 805	$98 805	$763	$228 966	$128 966
12%	$951	$228 402	$128 402	$894	$269 343	$168 343

   a) Explain why borrowers seek to obtain the lowest possible interest rate.

   _____

   _____

   b) What is the advantage of repaying the mortgage over a shorter amortization (*repayment*) period?

   _____

   _____

   c) What is the advantage of repaying the mortgage over a longer amortization period?

   _____

   _____

3.   Is it preferable to rent or to buy a house? What would be your advice in each of the following cases?

a) Alice and Dirk graduated from university three years ago. They found good jobs and have been able to save $10 000. Alice wants to start a family and she likes some new townhouses that are being constructed. They cost $105 000. Dirk expects to be transferred to another city within the next three years.

What would you recommend? Give your reasons.

_____

_____

_____

_____

_____

_____

b) Richard has just bought a small business in a suburban community. It is the kind of challenge he enjoys and his family likes the community. He still has enough financial resources to be able to make a $20 000 down payment, but this would leave him without a cushion if there should be an emergency in the business. The business yields an average net income of about $1 500 a week.

After looking at various possible homes, Richard and his family have a choice:

   • to rent a large house in an expensive neighbourhood for $900 a month

   • to buy a new house with four bedrooms and an in-ground pool for $150 000

   • to buy an existing home in an established neighbourhood for $105 000

What do you recommend? Why?

_____

_____

_____

_____

_____

_____

_____

_____

_____

Debt

OUTLINE

Debt is money owed. When a consumer obtains credit there is a debt to repay and the consumer becomes a **debtor**. The financial institution or the retailer who extends the credit to the consumer becomes the **creditor**.

Short term debts that are within the consumer's capacity to repay are not a problem. They are considered a wise use of credit. Most people pay them off at the end of each week or month. -e.g. telephone, milk, papers, gasoline bill, charge accounts, personal loans, credit card accounts.

"Running into debt" implies borrowing money beyond one's ability to repay the debt. This **over-indebtedness** represents the misuse of credit. Main causes are:
- impulse buying on easy credit terms
- careless budget planning
- over-extending the credit limit
- having too many consumer loans from a number of creditors
- protracted illness or long term disability
- loss of job, layoff, wage cutback, strike

Possible ways of dealing with outstanding debts
- **Design a personal plan** - with advice or financial counselling if necessary.
  - Make a strict budget plan with reduced expenditures.
  - Obtain a personal loan (if possible) to **consolidate** *(unite)* debts at a lower interest rate. The loan is used to pay off as many smaller debts as possible since most have higher rates of interest. Repayments are regular and the debtor keeps his/her property.
  - Destroy credit cards.
  - Sell some assets.
  - Renegotiate the terms of a loan contract with the creditor.
  - Find way(s) to increase income.

- **Repossession** - the creditor takes back the goods.
  - All payments made to date are lost to the consumer.
  - The debt no longer exists.

- **Voluntary deposit** - debtor arranges to deposit a percentage of his income with the *Services des dépôts volontaires* at the Provincial Court.
  - Exists only in Québec.
  - Prevents seizure of personal property.
  - Debtor or his lawyer registers with the *Services des dépôts volontaires* and gives all pertinent information.
  - Officials take into account the personal situation of the debtor and determine what percentage of his income must be deposited.
  - Money deposited is used to pay off outstanding debts gradually.

- **Personal bankruptcy** - debtor admits outstanding debts cannot be repaid
  - Debts total more than the debtor's assets.
  - Debtor turns over most of his property to a bankruptcy court or a trustee - bank accounts, car, house, furniture in excess of a value of $4000, but may keep necessities and tools required for his professional activities.
  - Court or trustee divides assets among the creditors (who must accept the decision).
  - Creditors only receive a part of what was owed.
  - Debtor is absolved of most debts (but not fines, student loans, alimony payments) and forbidden to incur other large debts while bankruptcy in progress (9 to 18 months). May make a fresh start once proceedings completed.

TERMS

Explain these terms in your own words:

creditor _____

bankruptcy _____

APPLICATION

1. Phil and Josée were laid off two months ago. They had been enjoying a good dual income and had bought many goods on credit to set up a very comfortable apartment. Now their savings are all gone but several payments are due each month. It is impossible to pay all their bills from their EI payments. They want to avoid having their possessions seized. What can they do to ease their predicament?

   Consider each of the following courses of action. Explain your assessment of each proposal.

   a) Sell some less important possessions to avoid having to make more payments on them.

   _____

   _____

   b) Consolidate their debts with a loan at a lower interest rate and a longer repayment period.

   _____

   _____

   c) Declare bankruptcy to avoid having to pay off their debts.

   _____

   _____

   d) Arrange to make a voluntary deposit and pay only a fixed minimum amount each month.

   _____

   _____

2. Bruno has been rising steadily up the corporate ladder. His salary is $2 500 a month. Because he was expecting a big promotion, he used credit to obtain an expensive sports car, buy a lot of clothes, and spend a month in a luxury hotel in Hawaii. Bruno now knows that he will not get the promotion for at least two years. He can pay his rent and the minimum monthly payments on his credit cards, but several creditors are beginning to push him very hard because he is not keeping up with his other payments.

   What can Bruno do if he wishes to reduce his debts and avoid any legal proceedings? Make at least two suggestions.

   _____

   _____

   _____

   _____

   _____

Personal budgeting

OUTLINE

A **budget** is an organized way of managing your weekly or monthly income and expenses. It is a statement of your estimated income and your probable expenditures for a given period of time - usually a week or a month.

Budget planning
- is the key to handling your money well. You know where you are going. It puts you in control.
- helps balance income and expenses and determine your **discretionary income** *(what is left over)*
- helps manage debts and major expenses
- promotes savings for future needs and security against unexpected circumstances
- makes it easier to monitor your costs *(identify how you are spending your money)*

The budgeting process
1 List your estimated income
   Include:
   - your **net income** from employment *(what is left after deductions for taxes and pensions)*
   - allowances and gifts
     interest from bank accounts and other sources
   - any other income from sources such as pensions, EI payments, investments
   BE HONEST AND REALISTIC. INCLUDE ONLY DEFINITE SOURCES OF INCOME.

2 List your probable expenses
   Include:
   - fixed expenses *(those which come on a regular basis)* e.g. food, transportation, rent, taxes, telephone, insurance. Some of these fixed expenses occur regularly in each budget period. Others are irregular and are often paid annually e.g. licence fees, car registration, life insurance.
   - savings *(Many recommend that you get into the habit of saving 10% to 15% of each pay to accumulate money for special projects.)*
   - flexible or variable expenses *(those which result from occasional consumption)* e.g. clothing, vacation, presents, entertainment.

3 Balance income against expenses
   - If there is a surplus you have discretionary income to save, to invest, or to use for fun
   - If you cannot make ends meet you have to go over your priorities and make adjustments to avoid over-spending. Flexible expenses can be adjusted to fit income.

Financial planning
- Is similar to budget planning but for a longer term.
- Helps you plan for what you hope to achieve or to acquire e.g. college education, car, house, vacation, retirement.
- Begin by establishing goals *(what you are working towards)*.
- Identify what you need to do to attain these goals.
- Develop a plan and keep records of your progress.
- Your plans should be flexible and adjusted as circumstances change.

TERMS

Explain these terms in your own words:

budget _____

_____

fixed expenses _____

_____

discretionary income _____

_____

APPLICATION

1. Prepare a budget for a fixed period of a week or a month. Use the lists below to guide you. Make changes or additions to suit your particular circumstances.

Net income	Weekly	Monthly
Earnings from employment		
Allowance		
Other		
TOTAL		
Expenses		
FIXED EXPENSES School lunches		
Transportation		
Savings		
FLEXIBLE EXPENSES School supplies		
Snacks		
Clothes		
Movies, concerts		
Sports		
Hobbies		
Gifts		
TOTAL		
BALANCE (Income – Expenses)		

2. Make a record of all your expenses for the past week.

   a) Which were planned and occur on a regular basis?

   _____

   _____

   b) What expenses were not planned?

   _____

   _____

   c) Was your balance positive or negative?   _____

   d) How might you reduce your spending?

   _____

   _____

   e) What did you do with your surplus (if there was one)?

   _____

   _____

   f) How did you make up the deficit (if there was one)?

   _____

   _____

3. Different age groups tend to have different goals. What do you think are some of the high priorities for members of each of the following age groups when they are planning their financial goals?

AGE GROUP	HIGH PRIORITY GOALS
14-17	
18-24	
25-34	
35-50	
50-65	
Over 65	

Other ways of protecting the consumer

OUTLINE
Individual action
The marketplace operates according to the principle of *caveat emptor* (a Latin term meaning *"let the buyer beware"*). This places a great deal of responsibility on the consumer.

Factors influencing your decisions include:
- your personal values
- peer pressure (*the influence that your classmates and other friends in the same age-group have on you.*)
- your family
- advertising on TV, on radio, in magazines and newspapers
- your age and your social circle
- your work and your experiences

Buying habits fall into two main categories:
- impulsive buying - unplanned purchases which result from desires and emotional needs
- planned purchases - bought after careful consideration of the product's use, desirability, cost, etc.

Consumer education teaches buyers to use the following process before making a purchase:

1 Establish your need
- Are there alternatives?
- Can I do without it?
- What is the **opportunity cost**? *(What must I give up the opportunity of buying to obtain this product?)*
- Will it conflict with other needs?
- How will I use it?

2 Select the product
- Select the styles and materials you prefer.
- Read as many information sources as possible.
- Research and investigate. Examine the product carefully. Find out what others think of it.
- Question several merchants and retailers about the product.
- Determine the probable cost.

3 Plan the budget
- Can you afford to pay cash?
- Will you need to use credit?
- What would your monthly payments be?
- For how many months will you have to make payments?

Collective action
Consumers may increase their power in the marketplace through collective action against producers.

- A **boycott** is a refusal to buy a certain product or service. If successful it can force manufacturers to improve the product or lower the price. Difficult to make totally effective.

- A **consumers' cooperative** can increase service and lower costs to members of the group. Owners are members who share in the management and operations of the business. A food co-op purchases goods in bulk and sells them to members at prices lower than those in the supermarkets.

- **Housing cooperatives** help members to enjoy lower rents and maintenance costs.

TERMS

Explain this term in your own words:

boycott _____

_____

APPLICATION

1. Think of a relatively expensive product that you or your family are considering buying or would like to have. Go through each of the recommended steps to help you make a wiser consumer decision about the purchase of the product. If possible, consult back issues of consumer magazines for informative reports on the product you are considering.

    a) Stage 1 - Establish your need.

    _____

    _____

    _____

    _____

    b) Stage 2 - Product research

    _____

    _____

    _____

    _____

    c) Stage 3 - Plan your budget

    _____

    _____

    _____

    _____

2 a) Did you ever purchase something that you really do not need and hardly ever use? What is it?

    _____

    b) What factors prompted you to buy it?

    _____

    c) What other factors ought you to have taken into consideration before buying it?

    _____

    _____

Consumer protection legislation

OUTLINE
Canada has a federal system of government. Consumer protection falls into areas assigned to both the federal and the provincial levels of government by the constitution. Each level legislates in its assigned areas.

Provincial legislation
The Province of Québec has the most advanced consumer protection laws in Canada. The *Consumer Protection Act* of 1981 contains over 100 provisions which are designed to eliminate:

- abusive practices
- fraudulent transactions
- misleading advertising

Contracts
A **contract** is a commitment between two or more people. Most are written agreements, but a verbal agreement is also a contract. Even a cash register slip is considered to be a contract. A contract involves rights and obligations on the part of the two parties concerned.

A written document is required by law for the following:
- credit contract - money loan, installment sale, issuing of a credit card
- sales contract with a door-to-door salesman
- sales contract for a used car or motorcycle
- leasing of services contract - language school, dance studio, dating agency, health studio

A contract must contain:
- the <u>date</u> when it is signed
- the name of the <u>place</u> where the contract is signed
- the consumer's place of <u>residence</u> if it is a door-to-door or mail order sale
- the <u>name and address</u> of the merchant (a post office box is not a legal address)
- a <u>description</u> of the goods or services contracted for
- the <u>total amount</u> you will have to pay. This includes all charges for delivery, installation, credit, etc.

In Québec the contract must be drawn up in French. However, if both parties agree, it may also be written in English. If there is a difference in interpretation between the two texts, the version more favorable to the consumer will prevail.

Contracts may be cancelled:
- *within 10 days* following the day when you receive a copy of a door-to-door sales contract
- *within 2 days* following the day you receive a copy of a contract for the loan of money or credit (except those made for the purchase of a new car that you have already taken delivery of)
- *at any time* and without charge for a leasing of service contract (excepting health studios) if the services have not yet started. If you have started, you must pay for services received and a cancellation fee.
- with a health studio in two cases only:
  - if you have not begun using the services, then no penalty applies
  - within a period equal to 1/10 of the term of the contract by paying 1/10 of the total cost of the services

YOUR FIRST RESPONSIBILITY AS A CONSUMER IS TO BE WELL INFORMED ABOUT LEGAL RIGHTS. SECONDLY, INSIST THAT THEY BE RESPECTED.

Federal legislation

The Department of Consumer Affairs - Industry Canada - administers laws that apply to the whole country:
- Food and Drug Act
- Combines Investigation Act
- Hazardous Products Act
- Consumer Packaging and Labelling Act
- Weights and Measures Act
- Textile Labelling Act
- Fish Inspection Act

Small Claims Court

In Québec residents may use the Small Claims Court to settle claims which are not greater than $7000. For a small fee the person making the claim makes his/her case before a judge. Relevant documents are presented as proof. The defendant may be present but no lawyers are allowed. The judge's decision is final, no appeals may be launched.

Warranties / guarantees

A **warranty**, also called a **guarantee**, is a contract by which the manufacturer promises to stand by the product if there is a problem. It says the product will serve its purpose for a reasonable period of time which is usually stated. There are different kinds of warranties:
- A *full warranty* states that the manufacturer will either repair or replace the product if it proves defective within a specified period of time.
- A *limited warranty* covers only certain parts of the product, or it may expect the customer to pay labour and shipping costs for repairs.
- An *implied warranty* is not given in writing but it is considered to exist in law if the product does not meet the minimum quality standards associated with that type of product.
- A warranty may be *excluded* provided you are told in advance of the purchase. You buy the item "as is".

APPLICATION

1. Pretend to be a wall-to-wall carpet sales-person who has just persuaded your parents to buy new carpeting for your bedroom. They want to have it installed by the company. Write out a contract which complies with all the requirements of the law.

Company _____

Representative _____

Customer's name _____

Description of items
to be bought _____

_____

Installation instructions _____

_____

Warranty _____

_____

Consumer protection agencies and organizations

OUTLINE
Public governmental agencies

- *Federal government*
  - Consumer Affairs - Industry Canada promotes competition in business through its *Combines Investigation Unit.*
  - deals with bankruptcies, corporate affairs, copyrights, and trademarks through its *Corporate Affairs Unit*
  - deals with fraudulent business practices, informs public about unsafe products, sets product standards, consumer inquiries through its *Consumer Affairs Unit*

- *Provincial government*
  - L'Office de la protection du Consommateur deals with most consumer complaints
  - deals with business practices, leased services, warranties, appliance repairs, advertising, door-to-door vendors
  - provides many free pamphlets and information on topics covered by the Consumer Protection Act

Private organizations

- *Automobile Protection Association*
  - Montréal-based organization dealing with complaints and information about private vehicles
  - advises members how to take a dealer or manufacturer to the Small Claims Court
  - publicizes secret car warranties
  - publishes a magazine: *Lemon Aid*

- *Better Business Bureau*
  - promotes fair business practices on behalf of both consumers and advertisers
  - will tell you if there have been similar complaints about a certain business operation
  - has no legal powers, but uses **moral suasion** to correct abuses

- *Canadian Standards Association*
  - promotes high standards of safety for a wide range of products, especially electrical goods
  - CSA seal can be taken as proof the product is safe to use
  - publishes a guide: *The Consumer*

- *Consumers' Association of Canada*
  - promotes wise consumer habits through education
  - publishes a monthly magazine: *Canadian Consumer*

APPLICATION

1. You have just taken over the "Dear Tubby" consumer advice column in your local newspaper. Write a brief reply giving accurate advice to each of the following requests.

   a) Dear Tubby,
       Yesterday I signed a contract with a door-to door vendor for a set of encyclopedias. They are going to cost me $550. Now I regret having agreed to buy the set. Is there anything I can do?
           R.B., Montréal

   _____

   _____

   _____

b) *Dear Tubby,*
   On January 15, Tudbury's advertised a well-known brand of swimsuits at "50% OFF". In fact, they were only $2.00 below the regular price of $39.99! I can prove it. What can be done about this fraudulent practice?

   Bertha, Pointe-aux-Trembles

   _____

   _____

   _____

   _____

c) *Dear Tubby,*
   I bought a VCR from our local store. It is supposed to have a 12 months guarantee on all parts and labour. When the VCR developed problems after six months I took it back to the dealer for repairs. He refused because I had failed to complete and send in the guarantee card to the company. Can he do that?

   D.D., Verdun

   _____

   _____

   _____

   _____

d) *Dear Tubby,*
   I've been ripped off. I took my car to a service station for a tune up. Because I was late for work and the service manager said it would take at least 30 minutes to make out a written estimate, I agreed to write "I renounce my right to receive a written estimate." on the work order. The bill came to $385 instead of the $50 or so that I was expecting. He did not phone me about the extra work. Do I have to pay for the extras?

   M.S., Hudson

   _____

   _____

   _____

   _____

e) *Dear Tubby,*
   I bought a six years old truck from a guy who advertised it for a reasonable price in your newspaper. He claimed it was in very good condition. It seemed OK when I took it for a short test drive. Now the transmission is shot and it will require about $1000 to fix it. Is the guy who sold me the truck responsible for the bill?

   Hopeful, Candiac

   _____

   _____

   _____

   _____

f) *Dear Tubby,*
   We are shopping around for a new wood stove. There are two we like: one with a CSA seal on it and another which costs $100 less. Should we make a saving or play it safe?

   L.M., Rosemere

   _____

   _____

   _____

   _____

g) *Dear Tubby,*
   I lost one of my credit cards last month. I sent an e-mail to the credit company the same day. Now they are billing me for $2 495 worth of purchases that I never made. Do I have to pay?

   Harold, N.D.G.

   _____

   _____

   _____

   _____

2. Interview someone who has recently had car repairs done. Determine to what extent the "letter of the law" was carried out in terms of the Consumer Protection Act.

3. Check some of the consumer advocacy columns in your local newspapers.

Savings

OUTLINE

Savings can be defined as *unspent income* or *deferred spending*. It is that portion of income that remains after all taxes and consumer expenses have been paid.

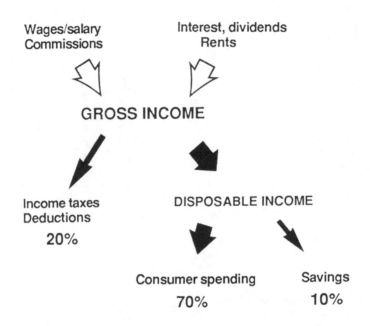

Reasons for saving
- *Build up funds for recurring annual expenses* such as car insurance, municipal taxes, insurance premiums. These payments are usually fairly large and can pose a problem if provisions have not been made to cover them.
- *Build up a cushion for unexpected emergencies* such as unemployment, strike, lockout, long illness, major repairs. It is often recommended that this fund be equal to about three to four months income.
- *Build up funds for large but infrequent expenses* such as a car, a fridge, furniture, a down payment on a house.
- *Build up a reserve* to be able to take advantage of an investment or business opportunity. Having some savings can often make it easier to borrow extra funds.
- *Build up a reserve to supplement retirement income* and pensions and thus maintain a standard of living. Many use a RRSP (registered retirement savings plan) for this purpose.

Benefits of savings
- Savings earn interest. They should be invested so that the interest they earn keeps your nest egg ahead of the inflation rate.
- Businesses can use the funds provided by savings to create new enterprises and modernize old ones. This produces more goods and generates more jobs. This increases the gross domestic product and leads to more consumer spending and economic growth.

TERMS

Use your own words to explain these terms:

savings _____

disposable income _____

APPLICATION

1. Some people keep their savings in jars or "piggy banks". Give at least two reasons why they should not keep their savings in these ways.

    _____

    _____

    _____

2. Suppose that you are counselling a friend on the merits of saving. Suggest three guidelines that will help to develop a successful savings plan.

    _____

    _____

    _____

    _____

3. Inquire at your local bank or caisse populaire about current interest rates being offered on their different types of savings accounts. (They are often displayed in the window or in the public area of the bank.) Complete the table below to record your findings.

Type of account	DAILY INTEREST SAVINGS ACCOUNT	PURE SAVINGS ACCOUNT	TERM DEPOSIT	GENERAL INVESTMENT CERTIFICATE (GIC)
Rate of interest				
Calculated how often?				
Paid when?				

4 a) Check the financial or business pages of your local newspaper to discover the current interest rates being offered by the various financial institutions in your area. (This data usually appears as a table in the Monday edition.)

   b) How do the rates offered by chartered banks and trust companies compare?

   _____

   _____

   _____

Investment of savings

OUTLINE
Factors to be considered when investing savings

- **Income** -The rate of return should be higher than the rate of inflation plus any taxes incurred.
- **Safety** or the risk involved - Most small investors want total security. High risk investments offer greater returns.
- **Growth** or the possibility of capital gains - Shares and real estate investments can increase in value and realize a **capital gain** as well as a dividend.
- **Liquidity** - How quickly can the investment be turned into cash?
- **Cost** - Some investments involve administrative fees, broker's or notary's fees.
- **Time** available - Some types of investments require more time and energy on the part of the purchaser e.g. supervising a stock portfolio, administering real estate holdings.

Types of investments used to deposit savings

- **Bank deposits**
  - Most people have one or more <u>savings accounts</u>. There are various types some of which have chequing privileges
  - <u>Term deposits</u> and <u>guaranteed investment certificates</u> (GICs) pay a higher rate of interest but the money is invested for a set period. The longer the period of investment the higher is the rate of interest. There is a penalty if redeemed before the date of maturity.
  - All bank and trust deposits up to a value of $60 000 are insured by the Canada Deposit Insurance Corporation, a federal government agency.

- **Transferable securities**
  - <u>Canada Savings Bonds</u> (CSBs) are just as safe as bank deposits, but they usually pay a better rate of return. They are completely liquid *(can be sold at face value plus accumulated interest at any time)*. Only offered for sale for a short period (usually late October and early November).
  - <u>Québec Savings Bonds</u> (QSBs) are very similar to CSBs, but the interest rates are a little higher and they are sold in early summer (May-June).
  - <u>Bonds</u> are issued by the federal, provincial, and municipal governments and also by corporations. Their face value at maturity is guaranteed as is the rate of interest. Bonds are traded on the market. The price depends on current rates of interest and the rate paid on the bond.
  - <u>Stocks</u> can offer more opportunity to make a profit but they are more risky than bonds. <u>Preferred shares</u> offer more safety because the dividend is determined when the stock is purchased. <u>Common shares</u> represent a higher risk but a greater potential for growth. There are no guarantees for the purchaser; if the company prospers, the shareholders may receive a dividend and the value of the stock increases because other people want to participate in the success of the company and are willing to pay more than the original price to obtain shares.

- **Mutual funds**
  - A **mutual fund** is a portfolio of bonds, mortgages, stocks managed by a professional staff. Investors pool their money with thousands of others who own shares in the fund. Shares can be bought or sold at any time at the current share price. The share price depends on the net value of the assets owned by the fund. Most funds charge a small annual fee for the services rendered. The main advantage of a mutual fund is the lower risk because the investment is widely spread and managed by professionals.
  - There are different kinds of mutual funds with varying degrees of risk and return. Bond funds deal exclusively in the bond market. Mortgage funds hold first quality mortgages. Both are relatively safe investments. Equity funds invest in the common shares of many companies. The risk is greater so the return is higher in years when there is not a sudden drop in share prices. International funds invest in foreign companies. Returns can be high, but so are the risks.

- **Investments that reduce income taxes**
    - <u>Registered Retirement Savings Plan</u> (RRSP) is attractive because it gives the investor a tax break. The amount invested is tax deductible up to a fixed limit. The investor builds a fund which provides money during retirement when tax rates are usually lower.
    - <u>Québec Stock Savings Plan</u> (QSSP) is a scheme to encourage investment in Québec-based businesses. The greater the risk, the more the investor can deduct on his provincial income tax return.

- **Real estate**
    - Buying a house is the biggest investment that most people make. It is a fairly good hedge against inflation because house values tend to rise over the long run. Capital gains made on the sale of a primary residence are not taxable as income. If interest rates on the mortgage are high monthly payments can be a burden. Maintenance costs, repairs, water and municipal taxes also add to the costs of owning a house.
    - Some people invest in income property as a means of making capital gains and earning rental income.

TERMS

Explain these terms in your own words:

capital gain _____

transferable security _____

real estate _____

APPLICATION

1. Below is a list of investments that are generally considered as either safe or risky. Use a check (√) to indicate whether the investment is safe or risky.

Type of investment	SAFE	RISKY
HOUSE		
SAVINGS ACCOUNT		
PREFERRED SHARES		
LAND		
GOVERNMENT BONDS		
COMMON SHARES		

2. In times of low inflation which of the following investments would you decide to buy? Give a reason for your choice(s).

Choice of investments:
- Bank deposits
- Canada Savings Bonds
- Common shares in a Canadian company
- Real estate (income property)

_____

_____

_____

3. Let us assume that the primary reason for buying shares is to receive a high rate of return. List the following stocks in the order in which you would decide to buy them.

NAME OF STOCK	MARKET PRICE	ANNUAL DIVIDEND
Oilwell Energy Inc.	$200	$5.00
Favorite Appliances Co.	$50	$1.50
Unusual Commodities Inc.	$80	$2.30
Québec Utilities	$15	$1.00
We Save Insurers Inc.	$60	$0.90

1 _____ 2 _____ 3 _____ 4 _____ 5 _____

4. Flo and Josh are retired. They have just sold their house and have moved into a retirement home. They want to invest their money so that it is as secure as possible even if that means a lower return. They also want to be able to use their money at any time if the need arises.

Which of the following portfolios best corresponds to their requirements? _____

5. Recently Pat won $65 000 from the 6/49 lottery. She has used some of her winnings to satisfy her immediate wants. Now she wants to invest the remainder in a way that will likely make a big capital gain in the next few months. She realizes that this may be risky, but she is willing to take a gamble. After all, that's how she got her money in the first place!

Which of the following portfolios best corresponds to her requirements? _____

Six investment portfolios with different types of objectives

1
- 20% in a regular savings account
- 40% in a 90 day term deposit
- 40% in preferred shares

2
- 20% preferred shares in blue chip companies
- 40% common shares in small businesses
- 40% shares in mining exploration companies

3
- 20% in a one year term deposit
- 40% in Québec Savings Bonds
- 40% in ordinary shares

4
- 40% in a regular savings account
- 40% in Canada Savings Bonds
- 20% in oil exploration shares

5
- 40% in a one year term deposit
- 20% in Canada Savings Bonds
- 40% in common shares in small businesses in Québec

6
- 20% in a true savings account
- 40% in a 90 day term deposit
- 40% in Québec Savings Bonds

Suppose you have been given a gift of $10 000. You want to invest all of it for the next year while you finish school.

a) What are your objectives for placing your investments?

_____

_____

b) How will you make up your portfolio with a variety of at least three different types of investments?

_____

_____

_____

c) Discuss your selection with some friends and evaluate its suitability.

Module 5

FINANCIAL INSTITUTIONS

&

MONEY

OBJECTIVES

5.1 *Compare the major savings and loans institutions.*

5.2 *Explain the phenomenon of money.*

The economic systems discussed in the previous modules involved the presence of a medium of exchange - money. This module introduces you to the phenomenon of money and to the financial institutions which have come into existence as a result of our use of money. Also examined are some of the problems which have developed, especially inflation.

Chartered banks

OUTLINE

Canadian **chartered banks** are those which have been granted charters by the federal government. These charters permit the various banks to operate in every province and territory in Canada. Their operations are regulated by the *Bank Act* which has to be revised from time to time to keep pace with the changing needs of the economy.

Characteristics of Canadian chartered banks

- They are **corporations** privately owned by shareholders. Shares are openly traded on the stock exchange. No single party is permitted to hold more than 10% of the outstanding shares in any one of these banks.
- Shareholders elect a **Board of Directors** who appoint a **Chairman of the Board**. They establish general policy and supervise management.
- Day-to-day management of operations is done by professional bankers.
- The **head office** is the administrative centre. It is divided into specialized sections responsible for credit policy, international operations, marketing, forecasting economic trends, etc.. Information and directives are passed on to the **branches** scattered across the country. There are thousands of branches of chartered banks in Canada.
- Each bank **branch** is a complete banking unit which accepts deposits and makes loans. Head office gives support to the branches, thus permitting individuals living in small communities to have access to the same range of services as those living in large urban centres.
- Bank branches also provide a wide range of financial services.

	Interest received on loans		**Interest paid on deposits**	=	**Profits**
-	*+plus+*	*-minus-*	*+plus+*		
	Charges for services		Salaries, operational costs		

- Profits are divided among shareholders according to decisions made by the Board of Directors

Services offered by chartered banks

Banks offer a wide range of services available at any branch or using electronic banking via the telephone or a computer on line.

- *Savings accounts* of various types - including *regular* (which allow chequing privileges and pay interest on minimum monthly balance), *true savings* (with a higher interest rate but no chequing privileges), *daily interest* (lower rate of interest but good if amount of money on deposit fluctuates frequently).
- *Personal chequing accounts* allow depositor to write many cheques for a flat fee per cheque or a standard monthly charge. No interest is paid, but customer receives a monthly statement and cancelled cheques. Some types pay interest on the balance over a set minimum deposit.
- *Commercial loans* form a major part of the chartered banks' business. Their best and safest customers pay the **prime rate** *(the lowest rate of interest available)*.
- *Personal loans* are available to low-risk customers with sound reasons for borrowing and some collateral. Interest rates are higher than the prime, but it may be possible to negotiate a better rate than the one first offered. Some customers can obtain a **line of credit** *(pre-authorization to borrow up to a given limit)* which can be used up to the limit at any time.
- *Mortgage loans* are made available to customers buying real estate.
- *Student loans* and *agricultural loans* which are backed by the government are provided to those who might otherwise be considered too high-risk.
- *Transfers of money* can be arranged through purchasing **money orders**, **certified cheques**, or **bank drafts** in Canadian or US funds, as well as other currencies.
- *Travellers' cheques* and *foreign currency* can be bought by those planning to travel abroad.
- *Automated teller machines (ATMs)* provide 24-hour service to customers with access cards to pay bills and to deposit and withdraw money up to a certain limit at times when the bank branches are closed. They are also used to pay bills and to make transfers from one account to another.
- *Debit cards* are issued for direct payment while shopping.
- *Bill paying services* are available for paying utility bills and other accounts. Fees are charged for these services, but they are free or reduced for seniors *(over 60)*.
- *Safety deposit boxes* are rented for storing valuable documents and belongings.
- *Credit cards* are issued for general purchases. *Visa* and *MasterCard* are issued by the banks.
- *Bonds, stocks, mutual funds, RRSPs*, and other securities may also be purchased through banks.

Security of the Canadian chartered banks

Deposits in Canadian chartered banks are very secure. Deposits up to a total of $60 000 in any one bank are guaranteed by the Canada Deposit Insurance Corporation. There was no bank failure in Canada from 1923 until 1985 when two recently founded regional banks in Alberta failed mainly because of unwise investments in the petroleum industry during the period when it was experiencing a collapse in the price of crude oil.

Bank ownership

Canada's chartered banks are divided into Schedule I and Schedule II institutions. Schedule I bank shares are widely held. No one interest may own more than 20% of the stock of a Schedule I bank and at least 75% of the ownership must be by Canadian interests. A Schedule I bank may open an unlimited number of branches. Schedule II banks tend to be subsidiaries of foreign banks. They are increasing in number.

In 1998 six Schedule I banks held over 95% of the total assets of Canadian chartered banks. They are often called "national banks" because their branches are found in most parts of the country. In 1998 the Royal Bank and the Bank of Montreal announced plans for merging into one super-bank. The Canadian Imperial Bank of Commerce and the Toronto-Dominion Bank then announced plans for another "mega-merger". There was opposition to the formation of such large financial institutions and the merger plans were abandoned after the federal minister of finance refused to give his approval under the provisions of the Bank Act.

APPLICATION

1. What are the names of Canada's large chartered banks at the present time?

    _____

    _____

    _____

2. Name some foreign-owned Schedule II banks which operate in your district.

    _____

    _____

3. What are the possible dangers in having just a few very large chartered banks in Canada?

    _____

    _____

    _____

4. a) Survey your family or some friends to discover how many of the services offered by branches of the chartered banks are used by them.

   b) What conclusion(s) do you reach?

    _____

    _____

    _____

5. The chartered banks all offer very similar services and their rates are almost identical. Give a reason to explain this.

    _____

    _____

Caisses populaires et d'économie

OUTLINE

A *caisse populaire* is a savings and loans **cooperative**. *Caisses populaires* are found mainly in Québec where about 9 out of 10 francophones are members. The movement was established in 1900 when Alphonse Desjardins set up a *caisse populaire* in a church basement in Lévis. Most *caisses* were set up in association with a church parish. Their members were often too poor to be able to obtain a loan from a bank. Now there are some 1 500 *caisses populaires* with combined assets comparable to those of some of the major chartered banks.

Characteristics of a *caisse populaire*

- It is a *cooperative* run on democratic principles. Each user is required to buy a share ($5.00) which gives the member the right to vote at general meetings of shareholders of the cooperative and a share of any profits that are being distributed.
- *Caisses* provide many of services offered by chartered banks and are considered to be *"near-banks"*.
- The members elect a board of directors, a loans committee, and a supervision committee to run the affairs of the *caisse*. These are unpaid volunteers from the community.
- Each *caisse* is **autonomous** *(self-governing)*, but it must comply with laws and regulations established by the provincial government.
- Each *caisse* belongs to one of 11 regional **federations** of autonomous *caisses populaires*. This enables each *caisse* to provide more and better services to its members.
- The 11 federations are united into a **confederation** *(le Mouvement Desjardins)* which acts as the coordinating body for all the *caisses*.
- The confederation provides services to all *caisses* such as:
    - making available additional funds for a caisse which is temporarily short
    - investing surplus funds of the *caisses*
    - providing computer services
    - training staff and administrators
    - operating insurance companies *(Desjardins-Laurentian Life Assurance)*
    - making industrial and commercial loans *(Investissement Desjardins)*
    - operating a trust company *(Desjardins Trust)*

Caisses d'économie

A ***caisse d'économie*** is very similar to a *caisse populaire*. In English Canada they are known as **credit unions**. They too are savings and loans cooperatives. Usually the members have a common bond; e.g. they all work in the same factory or belong to the same union. They have the same autonomy and organization as the caisses populaires. They are also united in a federation.

TERMS

Explain these terms in your own words:

autonomous   _____

_____

confederation   _____

_____

APPLICATION

1. Complete the table below to compare chartered banks and caisses populaires.

		CHARTERED BANKS	CAISSES POPULAIRES
a)	Where are they found in Canada?	every province and territory in Canada.	Québec
b)	Who are the owners?	shareholders	the members ?
c)	How is the Board of Directors selected?	elected shareholders	elected unpaid volunteers from the community
d)	At what level are local operations directed, controlled. and supervised?	the head of office is the administrative centre	locally (members)
e)	How is the local branch or caisse linked to other units in the organization?	Each branch is a complete banking unit, but the head office gives them support, information and direct the branches	through the federations which are linked to the confederations
f)	What services are offered to customers?	• various types of loans • various types of savings • personal chequing accounts	savings accounts loans, transfer of money credit cards
g)	Who is entitled to share in the profits?	shareholder	the members & shareholders
h)	Which level of government is responsible for laws governing operations?	federal government	provincial

2. Consider the following clues:

- Sylvie works in the parts department and Tom in the shipping department of a large company.

- Tom has been a member for five years. Sylvie joined only last year.

- They are both saving money to get a down payment for a house of their own.

- Each pay day, some money is automatically deposited in their account.

- In September Tom was elected to be a member of the board of directors.

- They hope to get a low-cost mortgage loan in about six months time, but first the loans committee must approve their application.

With what type of financial institution are they dealing? _____Caisse Populaire_____

3. Use the labels listed beside each of the charts below to distinguish between the organizational structure of chartered banks and caisses populaires.

a) CHARTERED BANKS

LABELS
Board of directors
Customers
Professional staff
Shareholders
BRANCHES

Shareholders

↓

ANNEAL GENERAL MEETING
Election of directors

⬇

Board of Directors

⬇

HEAD OFFICE

Professional staff

BRANCHES

Customers

b) CAISSES POPULAIRES

Confederation

⇧

FEDERATION

⇧

Professional Staff

| Loans Committee | Supervision committee | Board of Directors |

⬆ ⬆ ⬆

Members

LABELS
Board of directors
Loans committee
Members
Professional staff
Supervision committee
CONFEDERATION

110

4. Consider each of the characteristics listed below and decide if it applies to a chartered bank, to a caisse populaire, or to both. Indicate your decisions by check marks (√) in the appropriate column(s).

	CHARACTERISTICS	CHARTERED BANKS	CAISSES POPULAIRES	BOTH
a)	Sells shares on the stock market	√	√	√
b)	Shareholders elect the board of directors	√		√
c)	Has the right to operate anywhere in Canada	√		
d)	Each branch is under the authority of head office.	√		
e)	All members have equal voting power at the general assembly.		√	
f)	Sells Canada Savings Bonds	√		
g)	Sells Quebec Savings Bonds		√	
h)	The customers are also the owners.		√	
I)	The Board of Directors make the important business decisions.			√
j)	Accepts deposits and makes loans			√
k)	Controlled by federal legislation			√
l)	Sells shares to raise money		√	
m)	Profits come mainly from interest earned on loans.	√		
n)	Most loans are made to industrial and commercial businesses.	√		
o)	Federated with other units, but enjoys complete local autonomy		√	
p)	Offers a wide range of services			√
q)	Grants mortgage loans to approved customers	√		

Other financial institutions

OUTLINE
In addition to chartered banks and caisses populaires there are other financial institutions that accept and accumulate savings and make these funds available to businesses, governments, and individuals for investment in the economy. These institutions are often referred to as **"near banks"**.

Trust companies
- *Royal Trust, Montreal Trust, Canada Trust, General Trust, Desjardins Trust* are examples. Control of each trust company has been acquired by one of the large chartered banks in recent years.
- Originally their main function was to manage **trusts** *(property being managed on behalf of an individual during his lifetime)* and settle **estates** *(personal property left by an individual at the time of death)*.
- Trust companies also offer: chequing and non-chequing accounts
                                    safekeeping of securities
                                    management and sale of real estate
                                    drawing up of wills.
- Trust companies make *loans* as long as they can be secured by acceptable collateral.
- Funds are obtained from: savings deposits
                                 sale of stock
                                 sale of guaranteed investment certificates (GICs).
- The rates of interest are usually higher than those offered by banks.
- Trust companies invest mostly in residential mortgages, but also in provincial and municipal bonds, and other securities.
- Most operate a branch system like the chartered banks so the same services are available across the country. In recent years many trust companies have been purchased by one of the chartered banks; for example Canada Trust by the TD Bank, Royal Trust by the Royal Bank.
- Trust companies are supervised by both the federal and the provincial governments.

Finance companies
- **Consumer loan companies** such as *Household Finance* lend money to the general public. Usually these loans are made without collateral *(something of value which serves as a pledge that credit payments will be made)* so the rate of interest is much higher than that charged by other financial institutions. Finance companies raise money through the sale of stock and by borrowing from banks.
- **Sales finance companies** such as *General Motors Acceptance Corporation* provide credit to finance the purchase of automobiles and other types of durable consumer goods. Retailers make a contract with the consumer and then sell the contract to the sales finance company which becomes responsible for collecting the instalment payments.

Life insurance companies
- In Québec important life insurance companies are *Desjardins-Laurentian Life Insurance, SSQ Vie, L'Industrielle-Alliance Compagnie d'assurance, Manulife Financial, and Sun Life Assurance Co.*.
- provide large numbers of people with protection against risks of accidents, long-term disability, and death. **Term insurance** premiums *(payments)* are lower but they include no savings portion. **Endowment insurance** premiums include a savings portion which grows in value as well as a risk portion which pays only in the case of death.
- accumulate funds for investment in the economy. Most funds are invested in mortgages and long term government and corporation bonds.

APPLICATION

1. Match the types of financial institutions listed below with one or more of the statements describing certain characteristics. Some characteristics may be applicable to more than one type of institution.

FINANCIAL INSTITUTIONS	NUMBER(S)		CHARACTERISTICS
a) Chartered banks	6,2,7,5	1	Protect people against risks for a premium.
b) Caisses populaires	2,5,7	2	Accept deposits
c) Life insurance companies	1	3	Grant high-risk loans with no collateral
d) Trust companies	4,7,9	4	Invest mostly in residential mortgages.
e) Finance companies	3,8	5	Issue credit cards.
		6	Provide 24-hour ATM service.
		7	Offer chequing services.
		8	Provide credit to finance purchase of cars.
		9	Grant most of their loans to individual customers.
		10	Invest reserves in government bonds and other securities.

2. Which of the following statements are TRUE of all financial institutions? Explain why the FALSE statements are inaccurate.

a) Financial institutions accept savings from individuals and invest the major part in the economy.

FALSE - they don't invest the money, they just make it available for other people to invest.

b) Financial institutions make depositors' savings available to businesses.

TRUE

c) Financial institutions are the main sources of consumer credit.

FALSE: Chartered banks are the main source of consumer credit

d) Financial institutions are controlled by federal legislation.

FALSE: Both federal and provincial legislation have control over them

e) Financial institutions all pay the same rate of interest on similar types of savings accounts.

TRUE

113

Creation of money by the chartered banks

OUTLINE

Money is a **medium of exchange** that is universally accepted in the country where it is legal tender. People have confidence in using it to effect transactions because it is backed by the government and financial institutions.

Functions of money

You will recall *(Objective 1.2.3)* that money facilitates economic activities in three ways:
- a **means of exchange** used to pay for goods and services
- a **standard of value** which enables us to compare the current values of different products
- a **store of value** that enables us to delay purchases and save because money retains its value, at least over a short period of time

Types of money

- Before there was money people had to use the **barter** system to exchange goods and services.
- Primitive societies used **commodity money** - shells, grain, cattle, beaver pelts, wives, slaves.
- Since ancient times more advanced societies have used **metal coins**. Since gold was scarce it was the most desirable form of money.
- To avoid the risks involved in transferring gold, bankers and merchants started to use **paper money**. At first this was backed by gold deposits. In modern times paper money is not backed by gold. It can be called "fiat money" because people trust it. It has value because people agree to accept it.
- As the banking system developed, the number, size, and frequency of transactions increased. This led to the growth of **deposit money**. People deposit cash and cheques in bank accounts. They write cheques which are drawn on the amount of money they have on deposit. Today about 90% of all transactions involve deposit money. (Coins and paper money are used for about 10% only.)
- Increasingly **credit cards** serve as money. The issuing institution allows credit to build up as long as the user has enough deposit money to pay the minimum monthly balance. Some economists forecast that **debit cards**, which involve an immediate electronic transfer of funds from the purchaser's account to the seller's account, will make cash obsolete some day. **Smart cards**, which have a chip embedded in the plastic, can be used to make transactions without having to use a PIN or password until the pre-determined amount is used up.

Role of chartered banks in creating money

Each day the many branches of the chartered banks receive deposits in cash and cheques worth many millions of dollars. In practice, they need only keep a fraction of these deposits on hand to handle withdrawals. This is termed the **fractional reserve** and the amount is regulated by the Bank of Canada as specified in the Bank Act. Since 1980 banks are required to keep a **primary reserve** equal to 10% of demand deposits *(deposits in chequing accounts)* and 4% of other deposits *(notice deposits such as savings accounts, term deposits, and foreign currency deposits)*. Most of this cash is deposited with the Bank of Canada.

In addition to the primary reserve, chartered banks must also maintain **secondary reserves** varying from 0% to 12% of total deposits in cash or **liquid securities** *(that is, stocks and bonds which can be easily turned into cash if necessary)*.

After having set aside the amounts of money needed to satisfy the primary and secondary reserve requirements, the banks still have enormous amounts of cash on deposit which they can use to make loans that will earn interest and make a profit. They can also use deposits to **increase the money supply**. This important function is closely regulated by the Bank of Canada.

TERMS

Explain these terms in your own words:

paper money _____

_____

deposit money _____

_____

primary reserve _____

_____

secondary reserve _____

_____

APPLICATION

1.   Complete the table below to show how chartered banks use deposits and loans to create money.

To make the calculations easier, assume that 10% of the combined reserves have to be kept to meet withdrawals.

HOW MAKING LOANS INCREASES THE MONEY SUPPLY

STEP	AMOUNT DEPOSITED	AMOUNT PLACED IN RESERVE	EXCESS AVAILABLE FOR LOANS
1	$1 000.00	$100.00	$900 00
2	$900.00	$90.00	$810.00
3	$810.00	$81.00	$729.00
4	$729.00		$656.10
5			$590.49
6			
7			
8			

TOTAL OF INCREASE IN MONEY SUPPLY AFTER EIGHT STEPS

_____

Creation of money by the Bank of Canada

OUTLINE

The Bank of Canada is Canada's **central bank**. It is different from other banks in several ways. It is known as the "bankers' bank" because its clients are the federal government and the chartered banks. Opened in 1935 as a private company, it has been entirely owned by the Crown since 1938. The *Bank of Canada Act* requires that it be managed by a governor, a deputy-governor, and a board of 12 directors. The governor has to have frequent consultations with the Minister of Finance of Canada about **monetary policy** and its relationship to general economic policy. The federal government has ultimate responsibility for monetary policy, but the central bank plays an important role in establishing and executing the policy.

Responsibilities of the central bank *(the Bank of Canada)*

- control the Canadian money supply
- control interest rates and credit conditions
- maintain orderly conditions in financial markets
- protect the external value of the Canadian dollar
- control the printing of new paper money and the minting of new coins and distribute them to the banks. Also collect and destroy worn-out bills.
- operate the deposit accounts through which flow nearly all receipts and expenditures of the federal government
- sell, administer, and repay government bonds and treasury bills
- accept deposits from the chartered banks and make loans to them when necessary

Monetary policy

The government's **monetary policy** is designed to <u>keep prices fairly stable and employment levels as high as possible</u> by effecting changes in the money supply. The **money supply** includes all the coins and paper money in circulation outside the banks as well as deposits in chequing accounts in financial institutions.

The Bank of Canada attempts to influence the economy by changing the money supply and changing the interest rates. The objective is to help the economy perform at what the bank and the government consider "acceptable" levels of unemployment and inflation. The Bank of Canada effects the desired changes in several ways:

- The **bank rate** used to be fixed every Tuesday for the following week, but it is now changed only when market conditions make it necessary. This is the rate the Bank of Canada charges the chartered banks when they borrow from it. The rate is determined by taking the average yield on Treasury Bills and adding 0.25% *(a quarter percent)*. The chartered banks usually fix their **prime rate** *(the one charged to their most credit-worthy customers)* about 1% above the bank rate. Mortgage rates tend to be about 2% above the bank rate and consumer loans are often higher depending on market conditions.
  HIGHER INTEREST RATES ▶ **less borrowing and decrease in spending**
  LOWER INTEREST RATES ▶ **more borrowing and increase in spending**

- The **secondary reserve rates** can be changed by the Bank of Canada to expand or contract the money supply
  LOWER RESERVE RATE ▶ increase money in banks ▶ more money to lend
  INCREASE RESERVE RATE ▶ less money in banks ▶ less money for loans

- The bank can engage in **open market operations** involving the purchase or sale of government securities.
  BANK BUYS SECURITIES ▶ **increase in deposits in banks** ▶ **more money for making loans**
  BANK SELLS SECURITIES ▶ **receives payments from deposits** ▶ **less money for loans**

- The bank can also use **deposit transfers** between government accounts and chartered banks.
  TRANSFER GOV'T FUNDS TO BANKS ▶ **increase reserves of banks** ▶ **more money for loans**
  WITHDRAW GOV'T FUNDS FROM BANKS ▶ **decrease reserves** ▶ **fewer loans**

- Finally, the Bank of Canada can use **moral suasion** to persuade the chartered banks to modify their lending policies in the best interests of the country. Thus, certain regions or certain industries may receive preferential loan treatment from the banks.

TERMS

Explain these terms in your own words:

bank rate _____

_____

money supply _____

_____

APPLICATION

1. Add approximate interest rates in the boxes below to show you understand the relationship among the different rates charged for different types of loans.

BANK OF CANADA	CHARTERED BANKS		
Bank rate	Prime rate	Rate for mortgage loans	Rate for consumer loans
10%			
7%			

2. Complete the table below to illustrate the effects of causing changes in the money supply.

	INCREASE in the money supply	DECREASE in the money supply
What is the effect on people trying to obtain credit?		
What is the effect on the amount of money in circulation?		
How does it affect the demand for consumption goods?		
How does this affect production of goods?		
How does this affect employment?		
How does this affect prices?		
What is the undesirable economic result if it is allowed to go too far?		

3. The Bank of Canada sells $3 000 000 000 ($3 billion) worth of bonds to the chartered banks and other financial institutions. The banks sell these bonds to their customers who use deposit money to pay for them.

Use the word *increases* or *decreases* to complete each of the following statements which describe outcomes of the Bank of Canada's action.

ACTION: The Bank of Canada sells bonds.

OUTCOMES:

a) This . . . . the money supply.

b) The number of loans granted by banks to consumers . . . .

c) The overall demand for consumer goods and services . . . .

d) Production in factories . . . .

e) The rate of unemployment . . . .

f) The general level of prices . . . .

4. Assume you are the Governor of the Bank of Canada. The Minister of Finance has just told you that the government wants the economy to expand. List four ways you can use to help to achieve this.

i _____

_____

_____

ii _____

_____

_____

iii _____

_____

_____

iv _____

_____

_____

The causes of inflation

OUTLINE
Inflation is a continual increase in the general level of prices. It reduces the **purchasing power** of money. In effect, inflation devalues the currency *(it is worth less in relation to other currencies)*.

Types of inflation
* **Mild inflation** *(under 4% per annum)* When the economy is healthy there is a tendency for prices, wages, costs, and profits to rise slowly. In general, purchasing power increases and the standard of living is improving for most of the population. This type of inflation is normal and acceptable.

<u>SMALL PRICE INCREASES</u> ▶▶ *Higher profits*   ▶▶ *More investment*
                              Wage increases   *Increased costs of production*
                              Increased purchasing power *Demand increases*

* **Severe inflation** *(over 10% per annum)* involves a sharp increase in the general level of prices and diminishing purchasing power for most consumers. Price increases become frequent, generalized, and self-perpetuating. Prices rise much faster than wages so the consumer's **real income** decreases and the standard of living declines.

<u>BIG PRICE</u> ▶▶ *Decrease in real income*   ▶▶ *Falling demand for products* ▶▶ *Lower prices*
<u>INCREASES</u>   *Diminishing purchasing power*   *Fewer jobs*   *Unemployment*

* **Deflation** occurs when there is a period of *falling prices*. The real income of consumers increases resulting in more purchases which lead to more production and an increase in employment. Thus, there is a trade-off:

    REDUCE INFLATION   =   *Increase in rate of unemployment*
    Increase rate of employment =   *RISING INFLATION*

* **Stagflation** was an unusual phenomenon in the late 1970s when Canada experienced a <u>stag</u>nant economy with rising unemployment and also high in<u>flation</u>.

* **Hyperinflation** exists when prices rise so rapidly that a country's currency becomes almost valueless. There is such a fear of rapidly escalating prices that people try to spend their money as quickly as possible. Triple digit inflation is possible. In recent years, Russia, Serbia, Argentina, and Brazil have all suffered from very high inflation rates.

Causes of inflation
* *Demand - pull inflation*
  Demand for goods and services exceeds productive capacity. Consumers are prepared to pay higher prices. Prices rise and the value of money decreases. Too much money chasing too few goods results in higher prices and decreased purchasing power.

* *Cost - push inflation*
  Costs of production rise if the prices of raw materials, energy, advertising etc., increase. Wage increases also drive up production costs.

* *Structural inflation*
  Sometimes marketing boards can raise the prices of products regardless of market changes. Professional groups such as lawyers and dentists can raise their fee structures by general agreement.

APPLICATION

1. People tend to expect inflation to occur. Consumers sometimes buy more than they need of a product to escape inevitable price increases. Workers demand larger wage increases than necessary because they want to protect themselves from certain inflation. Investors want high returns to compensate for the sagging purchasing power of the dollar. These tendencies are all part of what is called the **inflation spiral**.

    Add labels to the boxes below to illustrate the train of occurrences in the inflation spiral.

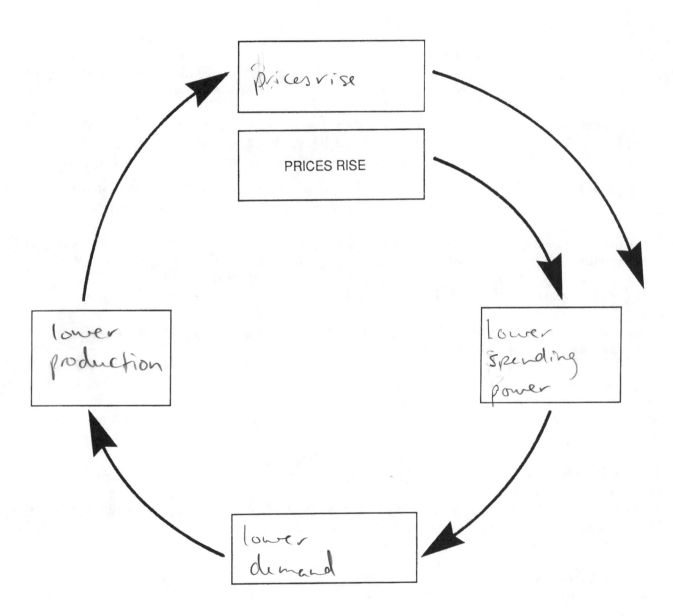

2. Which of the following situations are likely to cause inflation? Give a reason for your decision in each case.

a) Thousands of young families are looking to buy houses but fewer homes are being built and most existing houses are occupied.

Inflation would occur because the demand for houses would exceed productive capacity causing inflation

b) Most Canadians start to save more of their income.

No inflation occurs because there is no scarcity of products or increase in production costs.

c) The world price for oil drops by $10 a barrel.

No inflation because oil is now cheaper so the production price is lower.

d) All government employees are given salary increases of 3% for each of the next three years.

Inflation would occur because the economy would become more prosperous

e) The Québec government decides to push ahead with a major hydroelectricity development project which may cost several billion dollars over a five year period.

Inflation would occur because of the increase of taxes and high demand for building materials.

3. Consider each of the following actions or situations and decide how it is likely to affect the total money supply and also how it is likely to influence the rate of inflation.

		EFFECT ON MONEY SUPPLY	EFFECT ON INFLATION RATE
a)	There is a general increase in salaries.		
b)	Wages and salaries are frozen for a year.		
c)	The Bank of Canada sells 20 billion dollars worth of government securities.		
d)	The government of Québec raises all taxes by 10%.		
e)	The chartered banks are asked to increase their reserves by 2%.		
f)	The government overspends by some 40 billion dollars a year.		
g)	The government decides to print 10 billion dollars worth of new paper money and uses it to pay off its debts.		

Dealing with inflation

OUTLINE
Measuring inflation

The rate of inflation is measured by the **Consumer Price Index (CPI)** which is calculated by Statistics Canada every month. Survey takers note the prices of a standard "basket" of nearly 400 items used by most people. This is done in 51 cities across Canada.

The CPI indicates how current prices compare with those in the base year. As of June 2004, 1992 remains as the **base year** used for calculating the CPI so the formula for calculating the CPI is:

$$\frac{\textit{Price of the basket of goods now}}{\textit{Price of the basket of goods in 1992}} \quad x \quad 100 \quad = \quad \textbf{\textit{CPI}}$$

The effects of inflation

- *Decreased purchasing power*
  - The dollar buys less than it did before. If prices rise more than wages, consumers can buy less.
  - This is particularly hard on people with fixed incomes, pensioners, welfare recipients.
  - Has stronger effect on people with low incomes and minimum wage earners than on middle-class people.
  - Hits non-unionized workers harder than unionized employees who can press for a wage increase (if they do not already have an indexation clause in their contract). Professionals and entrepreneurs can raise fees and prices.
  - Many wage scales, pensions, and allocations are now subject to **indexation** *(if the CPI rises above an agreed level payments will be increased automatically to counter the effects of inflation).*

- *Discouraging economic conditions*
  - People have less surplus income to save, or they have to use some of their savings. There is less money for investment purposes so interest rates rise.
  - Inflation rates rise faster than interest rates and this discourages saving.
  - Sales decline, production slows or ceases, lay-offs and shut-downs are common.
  - Prices may become so high that products are no longer competitive on export markets.
  - Unemployment increases.

Controlling inflation

Workers, businesses, and governments all play a role in causing inflation. To combat inflation they need to work together, but this is not easily achieved because their interests are conflicting. Who speaks for non-unionized workers? Who represents small businesses? How do the different levels of government harmonize their priorities? How can consumers have input?

Governments try to control inflation in two main ways:
- *tight monetary policy* - decrease the amount of money in circulation by raising interest rates and thus reducing the demand for loans.
- *tight fiscal policy*- governments draw up a tight budget and cut back on projects and existing government expenditures. Governments can reduce consumer spending by raising taxes.

Other means of reducing inflation include:
- *voluntary restraint* - asking wage earners to reduce wage demands and businessmen to hold or cut prices. This is very hard to achieve and has proven ineffective to date.
- *control prices and incomes*- setting guidelines and limits for increases. This is easier to do for incomes than for prices. Requires a large bureaucratic organization to supervise the controls. Some commodity prices cannot be controlled because they depend on the international price which is set outside Canada.
- *freeze prices and incomes* - can be made to work for a short period of time. Prices and incomes tend to rise rapidly once freeze is lifted.

APPLICATION

1. How would severe inflation affect the lives of each of the following?

   a) Pensioners on a fixed income derived from rents, investments, and bonds.

   _____

   b) A worker whose wages are fully indexed to the Consumer Price Index.

   _____

   c) An investor who bought a 5-year GIC (Guaranteed Investment Certificate) that pays interest of 8% per annum while the inflation rate is 14%.

   _____

   d) A businessman who borrowed $500 000 at 10% to set up production of a new product that is proving very popular.

   _____

   e) A worker in a luxury product industry who does not belong to the union.

   _____

   f) A bill collection agency.

   _____

2. Which of the following measures would have the effect of slowing down inflation?

	YES	NO
a) an increase in income taxes		
b) an increase in bank reserves		
c) the repurchase of government bonds		
d) an increase in the bank rate		
e) a decrease in transfer payments to depressed regions		
f) a price freeze for two years		

3. Between July 1980 and July 1981 the bank rate gradually rose from 10.18% to 19.89%. This was part of the federal government's policy to combat the increasing inflation rate.

   Which of the following would increase as a result of this big jump in the bank rate?

	YES	NO
a) interest rates		
b) number of loans granted		
c) unemployment rates		
d) volume of production		
e) demand for consumer goods		

Module 6

GOVERNMENT

&

PUBLIC FINANCES

OBJECTIVES

6.1   *Show that the government has a role to play in the economy.*

6.2   *Explain how the budget is the government's principal means of action.*

The federal and provincial governments play a vital role in the Canadian economy. This module discusses the means used by governments to attempt to provide economic growth and stability. Governments affect economic growth through the allocation of resources, the redistribution of income, and monetary and fiscal policy. The revenues needed to pay for government projects have to be raised through taxation. For many years most government budgets had a large annual deficit which accumulated into an increasingly large public debt.

Allocation of resources

OUTLINE

In Canada the **market system** makes most of the basic decisions about production and distribution. When Canada instituted a federal system of government in 1867, governments played a small role in the economy. (Customs duties were enough to pay for all federal government expenses!) Since then, and especially since the great social problems that occurred during the Depression years of the 1930s, there have been more and more demands for governments to **intervene** in the economy. Today, governments spend nearly half of the gross domestic product.

Governments supply **collective goods and services** *(goods and services that the private sector is not so well suited to provide)*. Some goods and services would not be supplied in sufficient quantity if governments did not intervene.

Levels of government

- **federal**
    - for matters affecting all parts of Canada
    - powers listed in Section 91 of the Constitution Act *(formerly called the British North America Act)*
    - responsible for national defence, currency, trade, railways, ports, airlines, post, etc.
    - has broad powers for raising money through taxes and duties

- **provincial**
    - for matters affecting all parts of a province
    - powers listed in Section 92 of the Constitution Act
    - responsible for education, health, mines, highways, culture, sale of public lands, municipal institutions, etc.
    - has power to raise money through taxes within the province

- **municipal**
    - for matters affecting one municipality *(city, town, village)*
    - powers given in a charter from provincial government
    - responsible for roads, water supply, sewers, garbage removal, recreational facilities, libraries, security *(police and fire services)*, etc.
    - has power to raise money through property taxes and licences

Ways in which governments intervene

- **public expenditures**
    - Governments provide services such as schools, universities, hospitals, clinics, garbage collection, police, armed forces, law courts, cultural institutions, etc. for the use of all citizens. Aim for optimum level of welfare for the community as a whole.

- **regulations**
    - impose restrictions (backed by government authority) that are intended to modify the economic activities of individuals or corporations in the private sector
    - administered by many government departments, agencies, and boards
    - some are <u>direct regulations</u> which control:
        - *price* - rent controls, telephone rates, taxi rates, utility rates, sometimes wages
        - *entry* - licences for broadcasting (TV and radio), trucking permits, taxi permits, licences for telecommunications (telephones and cable TV)
        - *output* - supply of agricultural products (eggs, milk, wheat) and natural resources (oil, natural gas)
    - some are <u>social regulations</u> which control:
        - *health and safety* - consumer product safety, occupational health and safety, pharmaceuticals
        - *environment* - air and water pollution, land use, resource development
        - *fairness* - misleading advertising, financial disclosures, protection against fraud
        - *culture* - Canadian content in broadcasting, foreign ownership, copyright

- **subsidies**
    - provided to help some areas with problems such as high unemployment, declining industries
    - include cash payments and/or income tax deferments and/or low rates for energy or materials to encourage new industries to set up in a district
    - set up job training programs
    - provide technical assistance (especially to small, new businesses)

TERMS

Explain these terms in your own words:

intervene _____

_____

regulation _____

_____

subsidy _____

_____

APPLICATION

1. The following is a list of items that have their prices regulated by one or more government agencies. Determine under whose price jurisdiction each item is found.

   Use these codes while making your responses:

   F = Federal   **P** = Provincial   **M** = Municipal   **J** = Joint federal/provincial

alcohol	___	cable TV	___	eggs	___
dairy products	___	gasoline	___	electricity	___
air fares	___	local buses	___	taxis	___
postage	___	telephone	___	property taxes	___
tobacco	___	water tax	___	car registration fees	___
dog licence	___	passport fee	___	import duties	___

2. List six things you have done or used today that are subject to government regulations.

   i _____

   ii _____

   iii _____

   iv _____

   v _____

   vi _____

3. Give examples of some recent subsidies or some other type of assistance given by each level of government in your area. Try to include a reason for the government intervention.

a) Subsidy or assistance from the federal government

_____

_____

_____

b) Subsidy or assistance from the provincial government

_____

_____

_____

c) Subsidy or assistance from the municipal or regional government

_____

_____

_____

4 a) What is meant by **deregulation**?

_____

_____

b) Give some recent examples of deregulation.

_____

_____

c) Should governments engage in more regulations that affect the economy, or should they have less control over many aspects of our daily life? What is your opinion? Give a reason for your response.

_____

_____

_____

5 a) Give examples of government intervention in the economy which you feel must be retained at all costs for the benefit of all citizens.

_____

_____

b) Give examples of some current ways in which governments intervene in the economy that you feel should be stopped or handed over to private enterprise.

_____

_____

Redistribution of income

OUTLINE

The aim of redistribution of income is to reduce the impact of great inequalities of income among Canadians. The system is based on *ability to pay* - the larger a person's taxable income, the greater is the percentage collected as tax. In particular, it provides *extra support* for those who are:

- permanently disabled and cannot work to support themselves and their families
- experiencing a temporary set back because of unemployment, accident, illness
- receiving insufficient income *(below the "poverty line")* because of large family, one parent family with small children, pensioners with no other means of support, etc.

Universal benefits *(available to all no matter what income level)*

- access to basic education at all levels
- access to medical services and basic hospital care
- old age security (OAS) payments for Canadian citizens 65 and over

Special benefits *(available to those who qualify)*

- child tax benefit (both federal and provincial in Québec) paid monthly to families with children under 18
- scholarships, bursaries, and student loans to help pay costs of education
- veteran's pension for those who served in the Canadian Armed Forces
- Canada pension (CPP) / Québec pension (QPP) for those retired workers who contributed to the scheme
- widow's pension
- pension supplement for those on OAS who have little or no other means of support
- company or government pension for workers who have contributed to the scheme
- employment insurance payments (EI) for contributors in the early months of unemployment
- welfare payments for those in particularly difficult circumstances with no adequate means of support
- tax allowances *(extra deductions)* for age, disability, children
- drug prescription insurance plan in Québec
- government controlled low rent housing for people on low incomes
- job training programs to help people obtain employment or upgrade their skills
- payments to registered Indians and Inuit because of special agreements concluded with their group

Transfer payments

- are taken from one government's revenues and given to another government to help pay for the services it provides

Federal ▶ provincial	payments to ensure that the quality of educational programs and health services is equivalent in poorer provinces to that in richer provinces
Provincial ▶ municipal	payments according to needs and size of local tax base to even out the quality of social services being provided
Provincial ▶ school boards	payments to ensure that quality of schools is approximately the same in all parts of the province
Municipal ▶ individuals	welfare payments to citizens in need to ensure they enjoy a minimum standard of living

APPLICATION

1. Which of the above-mentioned special benefits would the following people be entitled to?

   a) A man aged 68 with a private income of about $25 000 a year who lives in his own house and paid into the QPP and company pension plans while he was working.

   _____

   b) A woman aged 32 with three young children whose husband died two months ago.

   _____

   c) A registered Cree Indian aged 22 who has not yet been able to find a steady job on the reserve.

   _____

   d) A man who served 25 years in the Canadian army before returning to a job in civilian life and who has now been unemployed for the last six months.

   _____

2. Which of the following schemes permit the government to redistribute income to individual citizens? Use a ✔ to indicate those which apply.

   a) OAS payments   ____   b) free education   ____

   c) medicare   ____   d) company pension   ____

   e) unemployment benefits ____   f) student loans   ____

   g) job training programs   ____   h) welfare payments   ____

3. For each of the following cases, decide whether the government's action is designed to stimulate economic development or to redistribute income to individuals in need.

   a) The government makes a $10 500 000 grant to a local school board to build a new high school.

   _____

   b) The government decides to give all welfare recipients the same amount per week regardless of age.

   _____

   c) The government offers guaranteed loan programs to small businesses.

   _____

   d) Hydro-Québec offers low rates for electricity to a company if it sets up a new plant in Québec.

   _____

   e) A city offers property tax exemption for 10 years to companies who establish in its industrial park.

   _____

The business cycle
&
the stabilizing role of governments

OUTLINE

The **business cycle** is a pattern of *highs* and *lows* through which the economic system passes over a period of time. The cycle is impossible to eliminate in a mixed market system.

When the economy is growing and expanding there is an *upswing* in the cycle. Businesses anticipate more sales and increase production. More people are employed and there is more money available for consumer spending. This is called a period of **expansion**, and if there is rapid growth it is called a **boom**.

When the economy is slowing down and experiencing negative growth there is a *downswing* in the cycle. Businesses anticipate decreased sales so they cut back on production. There are fewer jobs and demand for many consumer products is reduced. Such a period is normally called a **recession**, but if the decline is severe it can be called a **depression**.

The business cycle

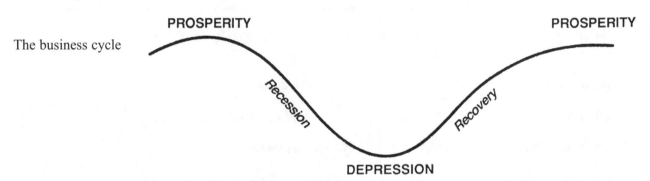

The stabilizing role of governments

Governments try to design economic programs to smooth out ups and downs in the business cycle so as to lessen their impact. In Canada, the federal government has greater responsibilities than do the provincial and municipal governments to try to stabilize the economy. Their aims are to:
- keep inflation down to an acceptable level
- maintain employment at an acceptable level *(under 5% rate of unemployment?? - but 8% rate may be more realistic!)*

Ways of influencing the stability of the economy include either or both:

- **monetary policy** *(using the central bank to control the money supply to influence the economy)*
  - increase the money supply to encourage demand and reduce unemployment
  - decrease the money supply to raise interest rates and slow down inflation
  - *(Refer to objective 5.2.1* Creation of money by the Bank of Canada *for more details.)*

- **fiscal policy** *(using the government's taxing and spending powers to try to stabilize the economy)*
  - can boost economy by spending more money *e.g. building new roads, schools, arenas, convention centres, hydroelectricity development projects, defence contracts, hospitals, office buildings, low rent housing projects, etc.* These all inject lots of money into the economy and thus try to stimulate a recovery.
  - lowering taxes results in people having more money to spend on consumer goods and services
  - conversely, if the government restricts its spending on projects and raises taxes, there is less money in the economy. The aim is to slow down growth.

- **automatic stabilizers**
  - Some government schemes work automatically to stabilize fluctuations in the business cycle. The government does not have to introduce them because they are already in place. They include:
    - *progressive income tax scales* - As people earn more they are taxed more; if they earn less they pay less tax and have a greater percentage of their income to spend.
    - *employment insurance & welfare payments* - add more money to the economy during a recession; inject much less money when the economy is expanding.

TERMS

Explain these terms in your own words:

fiscal policy _____

_____

recession _____

_____

depression _____

_____

APPLICATION

1. Show that you understand what is happening in each stage of the business cycle by completing each of the boxes in the table below. Always choose your response from one of these pairs of words:

high — low   *many — few*   *rising — falling*   *increasing — decreasing*   *large — small*

THE   BUSINESS   CYCLE

	PROSPERITY Peak / Boom	RECESSION Contraction	DEPRESSION Trough / Bust	RECOVERY Expansion
Production	*high*	*falling*	*low*	*increasing*
Prices				
Employment				
Wages				
Strikes				
Bankruptcies				
Bank deposits				
Bank loans				
Interest rates				

2. Refer to the financial / business section of a newspaper. Decide where our present economic situation lies in the business cycle.

a) What is your conclusion? _____

b) List some indicators that led you to that conclusion.

_____

_____

_____

_____

_____

_____

3. Concerned about high unemployment levels, the government decides to implement policies that should lead to the creation of jobs.

Outline its policies by using either the word *increase* or the word *decrease* to complete each of the following flow charts.

. . . .
in government spending
▼

. . . .
in production
▼

. . . .
in number of jobs

. . . .
in taxes
▼

. . . .
in personal disposable income
▼

. . . .
in consumption
▼

. . . .
in production
▼

. . . .
in number of jobs

4. Another government concerned about the possibility of galloping inflation decides to change its fiscal policies.

Outline its policies by using either the word *increase* or the word *decrease* to complete each of the following flow charts.

. . . .
in government spending
▼

. . . .
in production
▼

. . . .
in number of jobs

. . . .
in taxes
▼

. . . .
in personal disposable income
▼

. . . .
in consumption
▼

. . . .
in production
▼

. . . .
in number of jobs

5. At which stage of the business cycle would a government be likely to implement each of the following policies? (Refer to the diagram on page 130.)

a) Raise income taxes by 10% across the board.   _____

b) Refuse to hire more civil servants to replace those who retire.   _____

c) Grant big subsidies to companies to set up high tech industries.   _____

d) Lower the bank rate.   _____

e) Adopt a new budget which lowers corporation taxes.   _____

133

Promoting economic growth

OUTLINE

Economic growth is the increase in the output of goods and services over a period of time. For the country as a whole it is measured as the percentage increase in the Gross Domestic Product **(GDP)** over the period of time after adjusting for inflation. As the size of the population is constantly changing, the **per capita GDP** is a more accurate indicator of economic growth.

As the diagram indicates, despite the swings in the business cycle, the trend is towards steady growth in the per capita GDP. This results in a steadily improving **standard of living** for most Canadians.

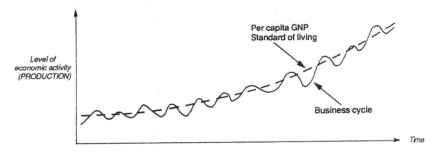

Canada's resources for economic growth

Canada has an abundance of resources. To develop them and thus promote economic growth, the various levels of government need to cooperate closely with labour and the managements of the many enterprises across the country.

- **natural resources**
    - include sources of energy, agricultural land, forests, fisheries, mineral resources
    - Governments can offer subsidies, low tax rates / tax exemption to encourage development.
    - Sometimes governments help to provide an **infrastructure** of roads, railway, airfield, energy supply to get an industry to develop natural resources of a region.

- **human resources**
    - the members of the labour force who do the work, provide the service, manage the operations
    - This labour force is constantly expanding, so it is necessary to try to create new jobs at all times.
    - Some members need to have their job skills upgraded to meet changing requirements.
    - Workers in declining industries need to be retrained to be able to find employment in other growing sectors of the economy.
    - Some need assistance to help them relocate in an area where there are sufficient job opportunities.
    - It may be necessary to find suitably qualified immigrants if there are not enough qualified workers in Canada to meet particular needs of employers.

- **financial resources**
    - Canada is a developed industrial nation with comprehensive banking and financial services.
    - Governments sometimes invest directly to promote a sector of the economy.
    - Governments may take measures to make sure that Canadian interest rates remain attractive to foreign investors. (If rates are not sufficiently attractive, there is a tendency for foreign investors to withdraw their funds from the country.)

- **technological resources**
    - Technology increases productivity by finding better ways to do things.
    - Many consider high technology and electronics to be keys to future economic growth.
    - Governments invest money in research and development *(National Research Council in Ottawa, Centre du recherche industrielle du Québec - CRIQ)*. They also encourage research by the private sector and subsidize most of the research being carried on in universities.

TERMS

Explain these terms in your own words:

infrastructure _____

_____

per capita GDP _____

_____

standard of living _____

_____

APPLICATION

1. Give brief descriptions of government schemes or policies to promote the economic development of the resources listed below. Indicate which level(s) of government is/are involved.

    a) Natural resources

    _____

    _____

    _____

    _____

    b) Human resources

    _____

    _____

    _____

    _____

    c) Financial resources

    _____

    _____

    _____

    _____

    d) Technological resources

    _____

    _____

    _____

    _____

Taxation

OUTLINE

To exercise their powers or functions, governments require **revenue** *(money coming in)*. **Taxation** is the main source of government revenues. According to the terms of the Canadian constitution, the federal government can levy direct and indirect taxes while provincial governments can levy only direct taxes. However, many provinces do levy indirect taxes such as a tax on gasoline.

- **direct tax** - is a tax paid directly by a person or firm upon which it is levied. Income tax, the goods and services tax (GST), provincial sales tax (QST) are examples
  - is not a "hidden tax" because it is calculated when being levied

- **indirect tax** - is not levied directly on the final consumer of a good or service
  - is usually paid by the final consumer as part of the price of the good or service *(e.g. taxes on gasoline, alcoholic drinks)*
  - is a "hidden tax" because it is included in the final price and not indicated separately

Federal taxes

- *personal income tax*
  - direct tax levied on the current income of the individual. It is a progressive tax *(Very low wage earners pay no tax, while people at the top of the scales pay close to 50% on their taxable income.)*
- *corporate tax*
  - direct tax levied on the current income of corporations
- *federal sales tax*
  - direct tax on most goods and services (GST) is paid each time a purchase is made
- *excise tax*
  - indirect tax levied on certain goods produced in this country which are viewed as being luxuries; e.g. gasoline tax, jewellery, tobacco and cigarettes, liquor, private aircraft
- *excise duty*
  - indirect tax levied on imported goods; e.g. machinery, wines, cars, clothing
- *capital gains tax*
  - direct tax levied on the profit made by the seller of stocks or property. At present, there are certain exemptions e.g. selling one's principal residence.

Provincial taxes

- *provincial income tax*
  - direct tax levied on individual earners. Québec is the only province which collects this tax itself. It is collected as part of the federal tax report for other provinces and then transferred to the designated province.
- *provincial sales tax*
  - direct tax levied on certain goods bought by the consumer. Some items are exempted from this tax in Québec e.g. books, medical services.

Municipal taxes

- *property tax*
  - is the sole tax that can be levied by municipalities. Therefore, municipalities need to depend on other sources of revenue such as provincial grants, municipal bonds, fees or licences, fines.

Kinds of tax rates

- **progressive tax** is based on the principle that the rich should pay a *higher rate* than the poor
  - Rates are automatically adjusted to the different capacities of individuals to pay.
  - The tax rate rises as the level of income increases.

- **regressive tax** is based on the principle that both rich and poor should pay the *same rate*.
    - The sales tax is the same for low income and high income people.
    - It is regressive because it places a heavy burden on the low-income groups who are less able to pay. To alleviate this problem low-income families receive a quarterly GST tax credit from the government.

- **proportional tax** is based on the principle that both rich and poor should pay the *same rate*.
    - The tax rate is the same for all, but its yield depends on the assessed value of the good. Municipal tax rates are the same for all, but the actual tax paid depends on the assessed value of the property as determined by the municipality. Owners of valuable houses pay far more than owners of modest houses.

TERMS

Explain these terms in your own words:

progressive   tax

_____

_____

regressive   tax

_____

_____

APPLICATION

1. Complete the table below to show which level(s) of government collect the various types of taxes listed in the first column. Use a check (✔) to indicate that the tax is collected by a level of government.

TYPE OF TAX	LEVEL OF GOVERNMENT		
	FEDERAL	PROVINCIAL	MUNICIPAL
Personal income tax			
Corporation tax			
Property tax			
Sales tax			
Excise tax			
Excise duty			
Licence fees and permits			

2 a) Conduct a survey with members of your family to discover how many of the different types of tax are paid by members of the household. Are there any that do not apply?

_____

_____

b) Try to make a rough calculation of the proportion of total income that goes to paying taxes of all kinds. Is it more than half?

_____

_____

3.   Complete the table to classify the various types of government revenue. Use a ✔ to indicate where each type applies.

Sources of revenue	TYPES OF TAXES				
	DIRECT	INDIRECT	PROGRESSIVE	REGRESSIVE	PROPORTIONAL
Personal income tax					
Sales tax					
Property tax					
Excise tax					
Licence fee					
Excise duty					
Corporation tax					

Tax reform

OUTLINE
Current problems

Income tax laws and regulations have become very complex. They occupy thousands of pages. Income tax forms are long and involved to the degree that approximately one tax payer in two now pays someone else to complete his/her annual tax return. Some people with high incomes are able to use loopholes in the regulations and a variety of tax shelters to avoid paying much income tax. Many workers operate in the "underground economy" where they do jobs strictly for cash "under the table" and then fail to report these earnings for income tax purposes. Sometimes goods and services are bartered. Some corporations have found sophisticated procedures for considerably reducing the amount of tax they have to pay. As a result, the present tax system is considered inequitable and many people have been suggesting tax reform for some years.

Possible reforms

- **Simplify and tighten up the income tax laws**
  - *Reduce the number of rates* and reduce the amounts that have to be paid.
  - *Close up most known loopholes* and discourage people from trying to cheat.
  - *Cut out most exemptions and tax shelters* to cut down avoidance of paying tax.
  - *Compulsory minimum tax* for corporations and people in higher income brackets.
  - Greatly *simplify tax returns*.
  - *Use the tax department's computers* to complete tax return for most taxpayers with an uncomplicated financial situation. Electronic filing of income tax returns is growing.

- **Modify the Goods and Services Tax (GST)**
  - The federal GST is a type of sales tax. It applies to most goods and services, but there are some exemptions.
  - Before the GST was introduced, federal sales tax was paid by the purchaser of the finished product. The government had to wait for its revenue till the good was sold. Moreover, it was fairly easy for companies to avoid including some of the tax in the price of the finished product. Some goods were exempted from sales tax for a variety of reasons. Services mostly went untaxed.
  - Since the introduction of the GST sales tax is calculated and paid every time a good or service is sold and exchanged from one producer to another. e.g. a farmer sells logs to a paper mill - tax has to be paid. The paper mill sells paper to a printer - tax has to be paid. The printer sells books to a bookstore - tax has to be paid. The bookstore sells a book to a customer - tax has to be paid.
  - The government collects tax at every stage in the production process. Each producer is taxed on the value added to the good as a result of his work. He deducts from the tax that he pays to the government the amount of tax included in the price he paid for the materials he bought to make his product.
  - Those who support GST say it allows the government to collect taxes sooner. It is harder to defraud the tax collector, and it applies to most goods and services.
  - Those who argue against GST say it requires a large bureaucracy to handle all the complicated paper work and administer the collection of the tax. Small businesses in particular find the paperwork expensive and time-consuming. Merchants blame the GST for some of the decline in sales because most customers hate to see 7% GST and 7.5% QST (Québec Sales Tax) added to the price of the good or service.

  Various ways of replacing the hated GST have been proposed:
  - a **business-transfer tax**; businesses would pay the government a percentage of their gross margin (total sales minus total costs).
  - a less complicated **retail sales tax** on all goods and services collected at the retail level only (not on sales between businesses).
  - a **personal-expenditure tax** collected through the tax return. The tax would be a percentage of the person's total income minus any money put into savings.
  - an **exchange of tax powers** between the federal and provincial governments. One level would cease to collect sales tax in exchange for grants or other privileges from the other.

- ## Increase corporation taxes
  - The increases would be passed on to consumers in the price of the product in most cases.
  - If taxes are too high in one area, some companies may be tempted to move away. Certainly, it becomes harder to attract new industries to the area.

(Continued on next page)

Is there a solution?

People complain of being over-taxed, but they expect the governments to provide many services, often free of charge. Revenues have to be found to pay for all these services and benefits provided by the government. If one type of tax (say, income tax) is lowered, then it will be necessary to increase the amount of revenue being produced by other types of taxes (e.g. sales taxes, excise taxes).

APPLICATION

1. Show how the GST operates by completing the following example. It assumes that the GST is 10% to make calculations easier.

TRANSACTION	PRICE PAID	GST 10%	CREDIT	AMOUNT SENT TO FEDERAL GOVERNMENT
A Douglas fir tree is cut down in British Columbia. It is sold to a saw mill.	$500	$50	—	$50
Lumber is sold to an entrepreneur who ships it to Québec and sells it to a furniture maker.	$1000	$100	$50	$50
The wood is used to make frames for armchairs. It is sold to an upholsterer.	$2000	$.......	$.......	$.............
The upholsterer sells twenty armchairs to a department store.	$4000	$.......	$.......	$.............
The store sells 15 chairs at the regular price of $400 each.	$........	$.......	$.......	$.............
The store sells the remaining five chairs at a sale price of $300 each.	$........	$.......	$.......	$.............
TOTAL GST PAID TO THE FEDERAL GOVERNMENT				$.............

2. If you were the Minister of Finance, what would you recommend to your cabinet colleagues as the preferred way to attempt tax reform? What are some of the possible reactions from taxpayers?

_____

_____

_____

_____

_____

_____

Government expenditures

Governments need **revenues** *(money the government takes in)* to help pay for their many **expenditures** *(money the government spends)*. Governments also draw up a **budget** *(plan for allocating funds to various areas of expenditure)* which is often introduced early in the year, but the Minister of Finance may introduce one at any time considered appropriate by the government. It tells how much and where the government plans to spend money during the year. It allocates funds to the various ministries and to services provided by the government.

For many years government expenditures increased substantially at all levels. This led to annual **budget deficits** *(the amount by which expenditures exceed revenues)*. In 1998 the federal government achieved a **surplus** *(revenues in excess of expenditures)* for the first time in 30 years. The surplus amount has been increasing in recent years. Most provincial governments aim for budget surpluses.

Increasing government expenditures

Some factors responsible for increases in expenses were:
- an increase in the number of civil service jobs *(government employees)*
- ballooning costs of social programmes such as medicare, welfare, education
- large sums paid in employment insurance benefits
- cost of high rates of interest paid on money borrowed by the government
- high rate of inflation which led to increased wages and prices.

Methods used to reduce government deficits

- cut-backs in government services
- lay-offs or early retirements for government employees
- salary reductions and salary freezes for government employees
- sale of crown corporations (privatization)
- increased taxes
- reduced transfer payments to lower levels of government
- tighter rules for obtaining employment insurance benefits

Budget for the provincial government of Québec 2004—2005

Revenue	$ millions	Expenditures	$ millions
Personal income tax	17 201	Health & Social Services	20 070
Contrib's to the health services fund	4 869	Education & Culture	12 460
Corporate taxes	4 248	Interest on the public debt	6 940
Retail sales tax (QST, fuel, tobacco)	11 899	Aid to persons and families	5 240
Hydro-Québec	2 040	Economy & Environment	5 600
Loto-Quebec	1 419	Government & Justice	3 980
Société des Alcools du Québec	601		54 290
Others (e.g. fines, natural resources, returns on investments, etc.)	6 940		
Sales of government assets	880	*No reserve amount to cover unforseen needs or a shortfall in predicted revenues was included.*	
Transfers from federal government	8 480		
	58 577	*Source: La Presse 2004 03 31*	

Budget for the federal government of Canada 2004—2005

Revenue	$ billions
Personal income tax	81.7
Corporate income tax	22.2
Employment insurance premiums	17.9
GST	28.2
Excise taxes and duties	13.1
Other revenues	11.1
Other income tax	3.3

Source: The Gazette 2004 03 24

Expenditures	$ billions
Direct program spending[1]	62.5
Transfers to persons[2]	40.2
Transfers to provinces[3]	30.6
Public debt charges	37.3
Surplus *(used to pay off debt)*	7.0

1 *includes Subsidies 20.1b, Defence 10.8b, Crown Corporations 4.7b, Other departments 26.8b*
2 *includes EI benefits 14.5b, Elderly benefits 25.7b*
3 *includes equalization, health and social transfers*

Transfer payments form a large portion of federal expenditures. Because they are tied to social programs and agreements with provinces, transfer payments are difficult to control. They include payments to:
- *persons*:   old age security pensions, child benefits, EI benefits, veterans pensions, etc.
- *business*: subsidies and capital grants
- *provinces*: equalization payments to allow poorer provinces to maintain social services at a high level, part of the costs of health insurance and higher education, etc.

For many years governments had large budget deficits. Now most have **balanced budgets** with some surplus in good years. Yet the amount of interest to be paid on the **public debt** *(outstanding debts of all levels of government)* remains cause for concern. Some of the surplus could be used to pay down the debt. An economy in a prolonged period of recession makes the problem more difficult to solve because revenues stagnate or decrease while social expenditures tend to increase.

Budgets for a municipal government (Montreal 2004—2005)

N.B.   This example is the budget for one city. Other municipalities could be significantly different in the amounts budgeted. Try to obtain budget data for your own municipality or borough if you live in a megacity.)

Main sources of revenue	
Property taxes	58.8%
Other tax bases	8.0%
Payments in lieu of taxes	5.8%
Other revenues from local sources	14.3%
Transfers	11.7%
Allocations	1.4%

Source: City of Montreal in The Gazette 2004 02 20

Expenditures by municipal function	
Public safety[1]	18.7%
Transportation[2]	15.8%
Environmental hygiene[3]	7.2%
Recreation and culture[4]	11.5%
Financing expenses	12.1%
General administration	15.0%
Health and welfare	3.2%
Urban planning and development	3.6%
Other	12.9%

1 *includes police and fire services*
2 *includes public transportation and roads*
3 *includes water treatment, sewers and garbage collection*
4 *includes libraries, arenas, pools, parks, cultural centres*

Municipal governments are required by law to develop a balanced budget.

APPLICATION

1. Compare and contrast the tables showing details of recent expenditures of the federal and provincial governments. What are the major expenditures at each level of government?

Major expenditures of different levels of government

FEDERAL LEVEL	PROVINCIAL LEVEL	MUNICIPAL LEVEL

2. Every level of government seeks to reduce its expenditures. Almost every solution has its disadvantages. What is the adverse effect of each of the following solutions?

   a) Cut-backs in the budgets allocated to operating schools and hospitals

   _____
   _____

   b) Lay-offs and/or wage-freezes for government employees

   _____
   _____

   c) Reductions in social benefits such as EI, welfare payments, pensions, family allowances

   _____
   _____

   d) Substantial increases in income taxes and direct sales taxes (GST and QST)

   _____
   _____

   e) Privatization of corporations and contracting out services now operated by governments

   _____
   _____

3. Which type of government expenditure has to be paid no matter what? What trend do you observe?

   _____
   _____

Public debt

OUTLINE

There are three possible situations:

- revenues   *equal*   expenditures   ►►►   **balanced budget**

- revenues   *exceed*   expenditures   ►►►   **budget surplus**

- revenues   *less than*   expenditures   ►►►   **budget deficit**

If governments spend more than they collect in taxes, they will have a budget **deficit** at the end of the fiscal year. This deficit must be paid, so usually governments get the money to cover the deficit by borrowing, either at home or abroad, or through issuing bonds.

The **public debt** is the outstanding debt of all the levels of government. It can be divided into:

- *internal debt*
  - This includes all debts owed to individuals and institutions in Canada.
  - It includes 30 to 90-day Treasury Bills *(short term borrowing)* and government bonds *(usually with a 20-year period to maturity, so long term borrowing)*. Both are sold to financial institutions by the Bank of Canada on behalf of the federal government
  - It also includes loans from the banks to the governments.
  - Citizens lend large sums of money to governments when they buy savings bonds. Canada Savings Bonds (CSBs) are sold in November and Québec Savings Bonds (QSBs) in June.
  - Québec government sometimes borrows from the *Caisse de dépôt et placement*.

- *external debt*
  - Some bonds are sold to banks and financiers in other countries; also, some loans are obtained from foreign banks.
  - Interest has to be paid in foreign currency. This can become a problem if the value of the Canadian dollar falls far below that of the currency of the lender's country. Loans acquired some years ago in US $, Japanese yen, or German marks are now very expensive to repay.

Justifications for the public debt

  - Sometimes governments borrow to finance public works projects *(e.g. new roads, sewage collectors, bridges, airports, schools, hospitals, filtration plants, etc.)* that will benefit many citizens for a long period of time. It is considered fair that future generations should help to pay for these loans.
  - During a depression or a recession governments may borrow large sums of money to inject them into the economy through various projects aimed at stabilizing the economy and promoting new growth. (This approach was urged by a famous economist named J. M. Keynes.) If this borrowing gets the economy moving and creates jobs, it is considered worthwhile.
  - Sometimes a government borrows money to enable it to pay its current bills for things such as interest payments, civil service salaries, unemployment insurance and welfare payments. This is considered to be dangerous. Lenders tend to demand high interest rates when the borrower is borrowing to pay existing debts. Moreover, it is considered unfair that future tax payers have to pay for borrowings which bring no benefit whatsoever to them.

The size of the public debt

The size of the accumulated public debt of the federal and provincial governments grew rapidly from the early 1970s to the 1990s. People feared a time could come when most of the GDP would have to go towards repaying the interest on the national debt. Governments saw the need for balanced budgets.

Governments were allowed to run up such astronomical debts because they are different from individuals. Governments go on and on, even if the political party in power changes from time to time. The country still has its natural and human resources and governments can tax the people more to obtain funds, or they can cut back on internal expenditures in order to be able to pay their creditors.

1. Complete the table to distinguish between personal / private debt and public / national debt.

	PERSONAL DEBT	PUBLIC DEBT
Capacity to pay		
Duration of loans		
Creditors		

2. Compare the data provided about annual deficits of the Canadian and Québec governments. In which ways do they compare?

GOVERNMENT DEFICITS OR SURPLUSES (+)								
(billions of dollars)								
	QUEBEC	CANADA		QUEBEC	CANADA		QUEBEC	CANADA
1976		5.7	1988	3.0	28.2	2000	+0.4	+12.3
1977		6.5	1989	1.2	28.9	2001	+0.022	+17.2
1978		10.6	1990	1.2	29.0	2002	0.2	+8.9
1979		12.5	1991	2.5	30.6	2003	0.7	+7.0
1980	2.9	11.5	1992	4.0	34.6	2004		
1981	2.9	13.0	1993	4.1	40.4	2005		
1982	3.0	14.9	1994	5.8	42.0	2006		
1983	3.1	27.8	1995	4.0	37.5			
1984	3.2	32.4	1996	3.2	28.6			
1985	3.2	38.3	1997	2.1	8.9			
1986	5.5	34.4	1998	1.1	+3.5			
1987	3.3	30.7	1999	+0.007	+2.9			

_____

_____

3. In your view, how will budget problems of the two levels of government affect the Canadian economy in the future? What needs to be done?

_____

_____

_____

_____

_____

_____

_____

_____

Fiscal decisions and economic responses

OUTLINE

Each year the federal and provincial governments prepare a budget showing their proposed revenues and expenses for the fiscal year. A fiscal year usually runs from April 1 to March 31 of the following year. In the budget speech, the Finance Minister describes the state of the economy, forecasts economic development for the year ahead, and indicates what measures the government proposes to stimulate employment and economic growth.

The government uses the budget to regulate the fiscal growth of the economy. In determining **fiscal policy** *(relating to government finances)*, the government must decide:
- whether to increase or decrease government spending
- whether to increase or decrease taxes.

Each decision affects the total economy.

- **increase in spending** ▶▶▶   *increases demand* for goods and services, <u>stimulates economy</u>, creates jobs

- **decrease in spending** ▶▶▶   *reduces demand* for goods and services, <u>restrains economy</u>, results in fewer jobs

- **increase taxes**   ▶▶▶   consumers are left with *less money*, reduces total demand for goods and services, <u>decreases employment</u>

- **decrease taxes**   ▶▶▶   consumers have *more money* to spend, increases total demand for goods and services, <u>increases employment</u>

Economic conditions and fiscal responses

The government might respond to economic situations as follows:

<u>ECONOMIC CONDITIONS</u>		<u>FISCAL RESPONSE</u>
High unemployment, recession	▶▶▶	High government expenditures OR lower taxes OR both
High employment, rising price levels (inflation)	▶▶▶	Lower government expenditures OR raise taxes OR both *In this case the government must be careful to ensure that attempts to reduce inflation do not cause serious unemployment. The major dilemma is how to wrestle the economic problems of unemployment and inflation simultaneously.*
Moderately high employment, stable price levels	▶▶▶	Little change is necessary.

APPLICATION

1. Think about current economic conditions and then:

   a) list some important indicators below.

   _____

   _____

   _____

   _____

   b) summarize current conditions with regard to employment and price levels.

   _____

2. Assume you are the minister of finance in a government. You are faced with the following economic conditions:
   - 10% unemployment rate
   - 8.5% inflation rate
   - expenditures have exceeded revenue by over $30 billion for the last four years
   - the national debt is over $500 billion and equivalent to nearly half the GDP.

   Here are some solutions that your advisers have proposed. Each has one or more consequences – both economic and political. What are they? Outline your response in the space provided after each proposed solution.

   a) Raise income taxes by 20% and sales taxes and import duties by 2%.

   _____

   b) Accept no new government projects, freeze hiring of new civil servants, freeze pay scales of all government employees.

   _____

   c) Reduce spending by 50% on all health and welfare programs which are currently responsible for about half of your total expenditures.

   _____

   d) Tell the central bank to print sufficient new paper money to pay off all of the existing public debt.

   _____

   e) Introduce tax reforms that include a business transfer tax and cut out all known tax loop-holes.

   _____

   f) Get rid of the armed forces and rely on the United Nations for protection.

   _____

   g) Refuse to repay all loans to foreign creditors.

   _____

3. So what would you recommend (other than resignation!)? Suggest an answer that might be given by:

a) an economist

_____

_____

_____

_____

b) a politician

_____

_____

_____

_____

4. What are some of the current fiscal measures being attempted by:

a) the federal government of Canada?

_____

_____

_____

_____

b) the provincial government of Québec?

_____

_____

_____

_____

Module 7

THE

INTERNATIONAL

ECONOMY

OBJECTIVES

7.1   *Show the importance of international economic relations.*

7.2   *Describe the economy of less-developed countries and their relations with industrialized nations.*

7.3   *Describe and explain the principal economic systems.*

This module will show the importance of international trade, in particular, the exchange of merchandise between countries. You will learn how specialization and trade lead to gains in total production and a general increase in standards of living. We will look at some of the reasons why nations want to restrict trade and how they take measures to hinder the free flow of products. We will also note the contrasts between the Canadian economy and economic conditions that are typical in less-developed countries. Ways of aiding less-developed countries will be reviewed. Finally, we will contrast the two principal economic systems found in the world until recently- our mixed market economy and collective economies associated with former communist governments.

Bases of foreign trade

OUTLINE
The buying and selling of goods and services in foreign markets is called **foreign trade** or **international trade**.

Exports are goods or services we *sell* to other countries.
Imports are goods and services that we *buy* from other countries.
   - A **trade surplus** occurs when a country sells more than it buys on international markets.
   - A **trade deficit** occurs when a country buys more than it sells on international markets.
The **balance of trade** is the difference (positive or negative) between the value of a country's exports and the value of its imports.

Canada usually has a surplus in the trading of goods with other countries, but we have a deficit in the exchange of services such as tourism, shipping, and financial transfers. In other words, Canada has a surplus in *visible trade* and a deficit in *invisible trade*.

Why do countries trade?
All countries have resources - natural, human, financial, and technological - but not in equal quantities. As a result, nations vary in their capabilities for producing goods and services efficiently. Just as division of labour and specialization can lead to greater productivity, lower costs of production and increased standards of living in a society, the same is true for regions, provinces, and countries. Consequently, it makes sense for a region or country to specialize in the production of those goods for which it is best equipped with the required productive resources.

However, if a region or country decides to specialize in the production of goods for which it possesses certain advantages, there are some implications:
   - There is an **opportunity cost** - the resources cannot be used for some other purpose.
   - It creates a need to **trade**. Foreign currency earned by exports can be used to pay for imports which include travel and vacations outside the country.

What should countries trade?
There are two possible situations:

- **absolute advantage**
  Each trading partner has special conditions which make it easy to produce a good in one country and very difficult in the other. Canada has conditions that favour production of wheat and paper products. Honduras and Colombia have conditions that favour the production of bananas and coffee. Canada is said to have an **absolute advantage** in the production of wheat and paper products, while Honduras and Colombia have an **absolute advantage** in the production of bananas and coffee. Obviously, it is to the advantage of these countries to specialize in the products which they can produce efficiently at reasonable cost and to trade with the other for products which they would find very difficult and costly to produce.

- **comparative advantage**
  Trading can still be advantageous even when a nation has an absolute advantage in many or all fields of production. The chances are that it has a greater advantage in one area than in another. For example, factories in the United States can produce computers and paper more efficiently than Canadian factories can. Suppose that American computer producers are 40% more productive than their Canadian counterparts, while American paper mills are only 10% more productive than ours. Then the Americans should specialize in computers where they have the greater **comparative advantage**. Canada would specialize in producing paper to allow us to earn enough US dollars to buy computers and other merchandise for which American producers have a distinct comparative advantage.

The principles of *absolute advantage* and *comparative advantage* clearly demonstrate that specialization and trade can lead to greater output.

Canada's principal trading partners (2003)
Figures are in billions of dollars.

	EXPORTS	IMPORTS	BALANCE
United States	345.2	239.2	91.8
Japan	9.9	10.7	-0.7
United Kingdom	7.6	8.9	-1.3
Other European Community countries	16.6	26.4	-9.5
Other OECD countries	12.7	19.8	-7.0
Other countries (not in EU or OECD) *	23.3	36.8	-13.5
Total for all countries	401.2	341.4	59.8

* *China is a major member of this group with $16.0 billion exports to Canada in 2002 and $4.1 billion imports from Canada.*

Source: Statistics Canada

TERMS

Explain these terms relating to trade in your own words:

absolute   advantage   _____

_____

comparative   advantage   _____

_____

APPLICATION

1.   List six products that we use almost every day that have to be imported into Canada because the foreign supplier has an absolute advantage as a producer.

1 _____   2 _____

3 _____   4 _____

5 _____   6 _____

2.   Using the same amount of resources, production of steel and plywood in the United States and Canada would be:

	STEEL (tonnes)	PLYWOOD (tonnes)
Canada	4	18
United States	6	20

a) Which country has the absolute advantage?   _____

b) For which product does the USA have a comparative advantage?   _____

c) Should Canada specialize in steel or plywood?   _____

3. Canadian workers can produce an average of 50 pairs of shoes and 20 sweaters a day. In Italy the average rates of production are 80 pairs of shoes and 25 sweaters a day.

Assume each country assigns 100 workers to making shoes and sweaters.

a) Calculate the total production per day if each country assigns 50 workers to shoes and 50 workers to sweaters.

COUNTRY	SHOES	SWEATERS
Canada		
Italy		
TOTAL PRODUCTION		

b) Calculate the total production per day if Canada assigns 100 workers to shoes and Italy 100 workers to sweaters.

COUNTRY	SHOES	SWEATERS
Canada		
Italy		
TOTAL PRODUCTION		

c) Calculate the total production per day if Canada assigns 100 workers to sweaters and Italy 100 workers to shoes.

COUNTRY	SHOES	SWEATERS
Canada		
Italy		
TOTAL PRODUCTION		

d) What conclusions do you draw?

_____

_____

_____

Free trade versus protectionism

OUTLINE

If we allowed pure **free trade** *(international trade free from all government restrictions)*, we would *import* our textiles, clothes, shoes, cars, and many other goods from countries which have a large comparative advantage over Canadian producers. To pay for these imports we would have to concentrate on producing for *export* those goods for which Canadian manufacturers possess a comparative advantage.

Advantages of free trade

- In theory, specialization and trade between nations can lead to greater output.
- Each nation is better off and the wealth of the world as a whole increases.
- Prices are lower because goods are produced at lower cost and there are no additional excise duties.
- Efficient producers have access to a wider market and this may permit even more economies of scale.

Protectionism

However, there are many existing barriers to free trade. **Protectionism** is a policy of opposing free trade. The main reasons why many countries oppose specialization and free exchange of goods are:

- **self-sufficiency**
  - Some protectionists argue that a country should avoid becoming too dependent on other nations, especially for its supplies of essential goods. *Strategic considerations* should take precedence over economic efficiency. Thus, some countries maintain an aircraft industry even though the Americans have a clear comparative advantage.

- **infant industries**
  - *New industries* need time to grow and establish themselves in the world market. During this period of time the government should aid and protect the young industry until it "comes of age". Some think our high tech industries need help against foreign competition.

- **protection of existing jobs**
  - *Foreign producers* can flood our market with lower priced goods mainly because their labour costs are much lower. They may also be using more up-to-date technology. If consumers are allowed to buy these low cost goods some Canadian workers will have to be laid off and, possibly, some manufacturers may be forced out of business.

- **need for a full range of industries**
  - It is not good to get too specialized producing only goods for which the country has a comparative advantage. What happens if a war or a trade dispute cut off supplies? And what happens to the workers in industries where we have no comparative advantage?

Means of protecting industries from foreign competition

When countries decide to protect their industries they resort to some or all of the following **trade barriers**:

- **tariffs** (Tariffs are taxes *(excise duties)* paid on imports to protect home industries.)
  - Tariffs benefit the Canadian producers but consumers have to pay more for the goods.
  - Tariffs were used to protect the textile and shoe industries which employed many in Québec.
  - Protected industries are often slow to modernize because they can shelter behind the tariff.

- **quotas** (Quotas set specific limits on the number allowed into the country of certain types of goods)
  - Quotas were used to restrict the number of Japanese cars allowed to enter Canada each year. There were quotas on imported shoes and textiles for many years.
  - Quotas can lead to shortages in supply and tend to raise prices.   *(Continued on next page)*

- **grants to support home industries**
  - Governments may give some industries funds to help modernize their plants so that they compete successfully once more against foreign competitors.

- **red tape and restrictions**
  - Administrative red tape, refusal to grant import licences, complicated docking and unloading procedures are used to make it difficult for importers to sell products on home markets. These all add to the cost of imported goods. Some goods such as meat products are prohibited for health reasons. It is a criminal offence to import certain drugs.

Branch plants are sometimes set up by international corporations in Canada to avoid *tariffs* and *quotas*. Because they are smaller, such plants tend to be less productive than those in the country of the parent organization so prices are higher. In other words, internationally they are at a comparative disadvantage.

International cooperation and global trade

Creation of trade barriers by one country leads to retaliation by other countries. International organizations have been set up to promote understanding, negotiations and cooperation in matters of trade.

- **OECD** *Organization for Economic Cooperation and Development* (based in Paris)

  Set up in 1960 to promote economic cooperation and development. Has 29 members, mostly rich countries. Produces valuable statistics and forecasts.

- **WTO** *World Trade Organization* (based in Geneva)

  An international organization of trading nations known as **GATT** *(General Agreement on Tariffs and Trade)* was created in 1948 with the aim of reducing tariffs and barriers to international trade. National interest groups protected by quotas, sheltered markets, high tariffs etc. opposed changes that result in freer trade. Agreements took many years to accomplish. Finally 131 countries agreed to establish the WTO on January 1, 1995. More powerful than GATT, it watches over trade agreements and has power to settle disputes.

- **EU** *European Union* (based in Brussels)

  The countries of Europe are gradually eliminating customs barriers and tariffs on goods and services. Twenty-five member countries form the world's largest common market. The euro is their common currency as of January 1, 1999. Member countries are also seeking closer political union. More countries want to join the EU.

- **NAFTA** *North American Free Trade Agreement* (based in Washington)

  On January 1, 1989, Canada and the United States entered into a Free Trade Agreement designed to promote a large free trade area in which tariffs and trade barriers would be gradually reduced over a ten-year period. Talks with Mexico resulted in the North American Free Trade Agreement which came into effect on January 1, 1994. Other nations such as Chile may join at a later date.

- **G8** The group of seven top industrialized economies *(USA, Japan, Germany, France, United Kingdom, Italy, Canada)* meet annually to discuss economic conditions. In recent years Russia has been present at the meetings to make it the G8.

Canada is a major trading nation. Exports account for more than one quarter of our GDP. Over half our trade is with the United States so we have **bilateral agreements** concerning trade between the two countries. The most important is the Auto Pact negotiated in 1965. Trade between the two countries is already duty free for most goods. (We still have to pay GST and provincial sales taxes on imported items even if there is free trade.)

There are also **multilateral trade agreements** among several nations which wish to promote trade and reduce trade barriers. Members of the EU and NAFTA have agreed to gradually abolish most trade barriers. Tariffs are being lowered as a result of GATT agreements.

TERMS
Explain these terms related to trade in your own words:

tariff _____

quota _____

APPLICATION

1. Assume that it costs $80.00 to make a pair of shoes in Canada, but an equivalent pair can be made for $50.00 in Spain. The government of Canada imposes a tariff of $32.00 a pair on imported shoes of this type.

    Complete the table to show the likely effects of both free trade and protectionism on each of the groups described in the first column below.

GROUP	FREE TRADE	PROTECTIONISM
Employees in a Québec shoe factory		
Employees in a Spanish shoe factory		
Consumers of this type of shoe in Canada		
Government of Canada revenues		

2. As a result of the free trade agreements negotiated with the United States, there are some winners and some losers on each side of the border. Protected industries stand to lose, while producers who presently face American protectionist policies gain.

    What is happening in each of the following cases?

    a) Canada's clothing, shoe, and furniture industries.

    _____

    b) Canada's producers of lumber, newsprint, transportation equipment.

    _____

    c) American branch plants in Canada.

    _____

    d) Canadian banks, newspapers, energy producers, civil service.

    _____

3. *"Even though a lot of people gain a little from free trade, a few people sometimes lose a lot."*

    Explain this statement. Do you believe tariffs and quotas are the answer to this problem? Why or why not?

    _____

    _____

The balance of payments

OUTLINE

Because of international trade and investment, billions of dollars flow into *(receipts)* and out of *(payments)* Canada each year. The federal Department of Finance prepares a statement of the **balance of trade** *(an annual summary of these receipts and payments)*. It distinguishes between **current account** *(trade in goods and services)* and **capital account** *(the two-way flow of investments)*.

The balance of payments indicates to what extent Canada's reserves of foreign exchange were increased or depleted during the year. If the bottom line is positive, there is a **favourable balance of trade**. When payments exceed receipts, there is an **unfavourable balance of trade**.

The current account

The current account includes **visible** and **invisible** imports and exports.

- **Visible trade** is concerned with merchandise which is tangible. *e.g. lumber, planes, computers, cars, shoes, clothing, books, TVs and VCRs, etc.*
- **Invisible trade** involves services and interest payments which are intangible. *e.g. payments for transportation, tourist expenditures, wages earned by foreign workers, dividends paid to foreign investors.*

Canada is a major exporter of primary products (e.g. wheat, forest products, minerals), so there is usually a large positive balance for merchandise (visible exports). However, Canadian tourists spend so much abroad, especially for winter holidays in the warm south, that there is a large invisible trade deficit. Payments of interest and dividends on foreign investments also involve a large deficit.

The capital account

Canada receives billions of dollars from foreign sources in several ways:

- Foreigners directly invest money in Canadian branch plants.
- Foreigners buy stocks and bonds of Canadian corporations.
- Provincial and municipal governments borrow money from the United States or Europe or sell government bonds there.
- If Canadian interest rates are high, foreign investors deposit currency in our banks - usually on a short term basis. (Normally, Canadian interest rates are kept higher than American rates to avoid this.)

Canada also spends large amounts of money by making investments abroad. If Canadians are attracted by foreign investments, there can be a net outflow of direct investment capital. Canadian banks make many large loans to foreign governments and corporations.

For many years, Canada has used a positive capital account to balance the deficits in its current account in invisible trade. There is a huge foreign debt owed especially to American investors and financial institutions. Some people are concerned about the extent of foreign control over our manufacturing industries.

Multilateral trade

The balance of international payments allows Canada to take its place in the world as a multilateral trader. Canada is able to buy goods and services from countries where it is most economical and to sell goods and services where it is most advantageous. If Canada were bound by rigid bilateral trade agreements, it would have to sell the same value of goods and services to each country as we bought from them. We usually have an unfavourable balance of trade with some countries, but we can pay using our favourable balance of trade with other countries.

Ultimately there must be equilibrium *(balance)* in world trade. The total of all exports must equal the total of all imports. However, it is not necessary that Canada must always have a favourable balance of trade or that she must avoid depleting her reserves.

APPLICATION

1. Match the situations below with one of the following transactions.

   TRANSACTIONS:

   | *Visible import* | *Invisible import* | *Capital inflow* |
   | *Visible export* | *Invisible export* | *Capital outflow* |

   SITUATIONS:

   a) A Canadian student studies in the United States on a Canadian scholarship. _____

   b) A Canadian immigrant sends a remittance to his family in his original country. _____

   c) Japanese-made cars are sold in Canada. _____

   d) A company in New England hires a resident Montréal business consultant. _____

   e) The Canadian government repays a foreign debt with gold. _____

   f) Canada sells gold bullion to a foreign country. _____

   g) A Canadian company sells its own securities in London, England. _____

   h) A Canadian company insures its goods with a British insurance company _____

   i) Canada sells natural gas to the United States. _____

   j) A US resident spends a vacation in Canada. _____

   k) A US investor buys bonds from a corporation registered in Toronto. _____

   l) A Canadian corporation pays bond interest to a US investor. _____

2. Analyze Canada's balance of trade with the following countries. Is it favourable or unfavourable?

   a) Russia _____

   b) United Kingdom _____

   c) Germany _____

   d) Japan _____

   e) China _____

Foreign exchange

OUTLINE
Why is foreign exchange necessary?

If Canadians confined themselves to domestic trade and investment it would be possible to use only Canadian dollars when making payments. However, international trade is an important part of our economy. Goods and services imported from a foreign country have to be paid for in a foreign currency. This means that the Canadian importer must sell Canadian dollars in order to buy foreign currency. On the other hand, a foreign importer of Canadian goods must buy Canadian dollars to pay for the merchandise. (Some currencies, *e.g. US dollars*, are accepted universally.)

The **exchange rate** is the price of a particular currency in terms of another. For Canadians it means the price of another currency expressed in terms of the Canadian dollar.

Because international trade is so important to the Canadian economy, our dollar has a **floating rate**. In other words, its value in relation to other foreign currencies responds to changes in the supply and demand for Canadian and foreign currencies. The exchange rates are published daily by banks and are quoted in most newspapers and on the Internet. Some countries prefer a **fixed rate** which does not change until the government sets a new rate of exchange.

The buying and selling of currencies is conducted on international money markets which are supervised by the world's banking system. The conversion of one currency into another is called **foreign exchange**. Government regulations affecting these conversions are called **exchange controls**. At present, Canada does not use exchange controls. Most of the transactions in the balance of payments are made by individuals or by private corporations and not by governments.

Why are exchange rates important?

If the Canadian dollar **depreciates** *(declines in value)* against other currencies, the prices of other currencies measured by the Canadian dollar will increase. In this situation foreign goods will become more expensive for Canadians to buy while Canadian goods will become cheaper for foreigners to buy. If the Canadian dollar loses value in foreign exchange it will help Canadian exports, but it will discourage Canadians from buying imported goods. Should the government want to create this situation it can devalue the Canadian dollar.

If the Canadian dollar **appreciates** *(increases in value)* against other currencies, the prices of the other currencies measured by the Canadian dollar will decrease. In this situation foreign goods become cheaper to Canadians while Canadian goods become more expensive to foreigners. If the Canadian dollar gains too much in value for foreign exchange purposes it hurts Canadian exports but encourages Canadian consumers to buy more imported goods. Should the government want to avoid this situation it can revalue the Canadian dollar.

Why do exchange rates change?

Exchange rates are affected by supply and demand for currency. If international traders and investors need large amounts of Canadian currency to make purchases in Canada, then there will be a tendency for the Canadian dollar to rise in value against other currencies. If we are buying too much abroad, or if investors are withdrawing funds from Canada, the value of our dollar will tend to decrease.

Sometimes international currency speculators will create a run on a currency in the hope of making quick gains. Their activities lead to artificially high or low rates of exchange for short periods.

Exchange rates - Canadian dollars in US dollars			
	Average		Average
1974	1.0225	1992	0.8276
1976	1.0141	1994	0.7321
1978	0.8770	1996	0.7331
1980	0.8554	1998	0.6767
1982	0.8103	1999	0.6730
1984	0.7723	2000	0.6733
1986	0.7197	2001	0.6458
1988	0.8124	2002	0.6368
1990	0.8570	2003	0.7135
Source: Bank of Canada			

TERMS

Explain these currency terms in your own words:

exchange rate _____

_____

devalue _____

_____

APPLICATION

1 a) Refer to newspapers and find the latest exchange rates for each of the following currencies. The Internet has websites which give the latest rates and convert currencies for you. A useful site is **www.xe.net/ucc** .

United States — dollar	_____	United Kingdom — pound sterling	_____
Switzerland — Swiss franc	_____	European Union — euro	_____
China — yuan	_____	Japan — yen	_____
Russia — rouble	_____	Kuwait — dinar	_____
Israel — shekel	_____	Australia — dollar	_____
Barbados — dollar	_____	Mexico — peso	_____

b) In which three countries could you enjoy a fairly cheap vacation because of a favourable exchange rate?

1 _____ 2 _____ 3 _____

2. Check the exchange rate for the US dollar. Is it a good / bad time to take a vacation in the United States?

_____

3. When Canadian governments arrange foreign loans it is usually agreed to repay the capital and make interest payments in the currency of the lending country.

a) What is the effect when the exchange rate of the foreign creditor country rises?

_____

b) What happens if the Canadian dollar appreciates against foreign currencies?

_____

4. Is it good for Canada when our dollar is valued well below the US dollar? Give reasons for your opinion.

_____

_____

_____

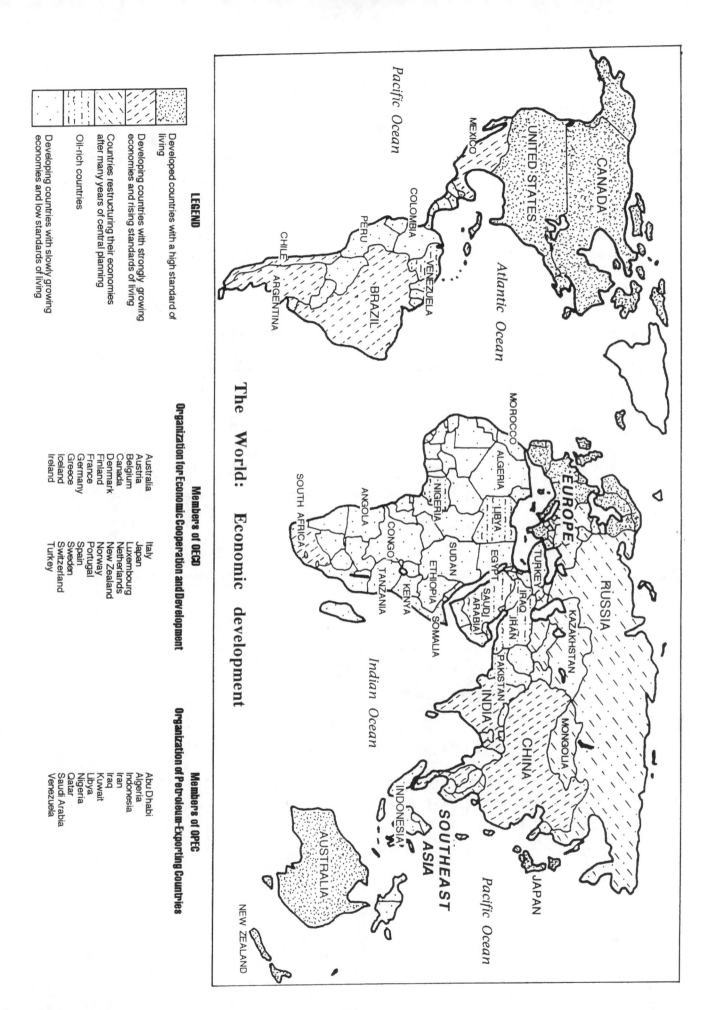

The World: Economic development

LEGEND

Developed countries with a high standard of living

Developing countries with strongly growing economies and rising standards of living

Countries restructuring their economies after many years of central planning

Oil-rich countries

Developing countries with slowly growing economies and low standards of living

Members of OECD
Organization for Economic Cooperation and Development

Australia
Austria
Belgium
Canada
Denmark
Finland
France
Germany
Greece
Iceland
Ireland

Italy
Japan
Luxembourg
Netherlands
New Zealand
Norway
Portugal
Spain
Sweden
Switzerland
Turkey

Members of OPEC
Organization of Petroleum-Exporting Countries

Abu Dhabi
Algeria
Indonesia
Iran
Iraq
Kuwait
Libya
Nigeria
Qatar
Saudi Arabia
Venezuela

The European Union (EU)

On the map above, use a colour or shading to identify the 25 member countries of the European Union.

Year joined	Member countries
1952	Belgium, France, Germany, Italy, Luxembourg, Netherlands
1973	Denmark, Ireland, United Kingdom
1981	Greece
1986	Portugal, Spain
1995	Austria, Finland, Sweden
2004	Cyprus*, Czech Republic, Estonia, Hungary, Latvia, Lithuania, Malta, Poland, Slovenia, Slovakia

* Only the Greek-speaking part of the island for the moment.

Characteristics of less-developed countries

Characteristics of developed countries (*also called* **MEDCs** - *more economically developed countries*)
- Most people enjoy a *high standard of living.*
- These countries have a relatively *strong and diversified economy* that no longer relies on agriculture as the most important contributor to the GDP.
- *Industrialized economy.* Most people live in cities. The transportation system is good.
- Basic needs are satisfied and enough resources left to be devoted to education, health care, and leisure activities.
- Per capita income is high. Food intake is high. Life expectancy is high. Most people have had some education.

Developed, industrialized countries <u>used to be divided</u> into two groups:
- **countries with a mixed economy** mostly in North America *(United States, Canada)* and western Europe *(United Kingdom, France, Italy, Germany, Sweden, Denmark, Netherlands, Switzerland, Spain, etc.)* but also include Japan, Australia, and New Zealand. Sometimes was called the **First World**.

- **countries with a planned economy** These included the former U.S.S.R. *(Russia and fourteen other republics)* and the countries in eastern Europe which had communist governments *(Poland, Czechoslovakia, Hungary, Romania, Bulgaria, Yugoslavia).* Today these countries (if they exist) no longer have communist governments and are struggling to introduce democratic reforms including *developing a free-market economy.* These countries used to be called the **Second World**.

Characteristics of less-economically developed countries (LEDCs) / developing countries / *(formerly called the **Third World**)*
- They *do not have the wealth* or the power of industrially developed countries.
- Many were once *colonies* of developed nations, but nearly all have achieved political independence. As colonies they supplied raw materials to the developed country which provided manufactured goods and technical know-how in return. The colonies did not build up a highly skilled labour force nor did they accumulate investment capital.
- Some are still *partially dependent on one major export resource* and are at the mercy of price fluctuations on the world market. *e.g. Malaysia for rubber, Cuba for sugar, Kenya for coffee.*
- **Low per capita income** is common. *(Per capita income = GDP ÷ total population)* This is partly due to the large numbers of young children in the population. Often close to half the population is under 18 years old.
- **Low literacy rate**. *(Literacy rate indicates the level of basic education within a country.)* It indicates the percentage of people who can read and write their language sufficiently well to be able to function in everyday life. They need these basics to operate modern businesses and to keep technologically advanced equipment functioning. Developing countries have restricted funds to allocate to education and large numbers of potential students. Because traditional farming methods often rely on much help from children, this also reduces the time available for schooling.   However, there has been considerable improvement in the literacy rates in recent years.
- **High birth rate**. Developing countries have high birth rates *(over 30 per thousand in some)* mainly because of cultural differences. Having many children enhances the standing of the parents. They also provide a cheap source of labour to help run the family farming plot and ensure that there will be someone to care for the parents when they are too old to work. Large families compound the problems of poverty and lack of higher education. Many countries are overpopulated *(i.e. they have too many people for the present state of development of their productive resources)*. Many workers are under-employed.
- **Low life expectancy** and **high infant mortality**. Many children die before the age of five due to poor nutrition, lack of clean water and sewage disposal systems, epidemics of various diseases, shortage of hospitals, doctors and drugs, inadequate housing. Hard physical labour also causes some to die sooner.

- Many still spend much of their time labouring to produce poor crops from exhausted land. Most of the work is done by women and children. These countries have a high proportion of their labour force working in the primary sector.
- Many rural poor are moving from the overcrowded villages to try to find better conditions in mushrooming cities. They are forced to live in crowded slums. Sanitation is very poor. Work is hard to find.
- A democratic system of government is now less rare. Some less-developed countries are still ruled by a dictator or a ruling junta. The ruling class is privileged and tends to get rich at the expense of the masses.
- Many spend too large a proportion of their GDP on buying weapons from the big powers.

Less-developed countries can be divided into several groups:

- **oil-rich countries with high per capita incomes** such as Saudi Arabia, Kuwait, Bahrain, Qatar, Brunei, United Arab Emirates. The rulers of these countries have vast wealth from oil revenues. Some is being spent to improve living conditions, but the countries are still in the developing stage.

- **less-developed countries with moderate per capita income levels** such as Brazil, Argentina, Mexico, Israel, Turkey, Taiwan, South Korea. There has been considerable industrial development, but there is a shortage of capital. These countries tend to have huge foreign debts and inflation rates tend to be high.

- **underdeveloped countries with low per capita income levels** such as India, China, Indonesia, most countries in Africa, southeast Asia, and South America. These are the countries where many have very low standards of living. They were sometimes referred to as the **Third World.** Some, such as China, India, Indonesia, have started to develop rapidly and will eventually join the group of developed nations. Others, such as Bangladesh, Mali, Somalia, lack the resources to overcome their many problems. These impoverished countries with little hope for a bright economic future were sometimes called the **Fourth World.**

(The terms First World, Second World, Third World, and Fourth World have fallen into disuse. The terms MEDCs and LEDCs are preferred. The distinct differences in levels of economic development remain.)

APPLICATION

1. Analyze the data presented in the table below and decide whether each country can be classified as a *developed country* or a *less-developed country*.

COUNTRY	PER CAPITA INCOME	LITERACY RATE	BIRTH RATE	LIFE EXPECTANCY	
A	$1 010	34%	50	48	_____
B	$270	23%	42	51	_____
C	$2 390	93%	25	69	_____
D	$13 520	99%	12	75	_____
E	$2 130	83%	32	65	_____
F	$3 900	98%	20	71	_____
G	$290	69%	22	65	_____
H	$300	24%	44	51	_____
I	$9 890	99%	14	76	_____

Relations with industrialized nations

OUTLINE

The basic relationship between the less-developed and the industrialized nations can be broken down into two main categories: **aid** and **trade**.

Aid to less-developed countries

- **food aid**
  - Developed countries send surplus food to alleviate food shortages or starvation.
  - Serves dual purpose of eliminating the surplus in the developed country and the shortage in the less-developed country.
  - Stop-gap measure that does not solve any of the basic problems of less-developed countries.

- **financial aid**
  - Can be a grant *(does not have to be repaid)* or a loan.
  - May have certain conditions attached to the grant to govern how the money is spent. Advisers and technical equipment may have to come from donor country.
  - Loans may come from an international, non-governmental agency such as the *World Bank*, or they may be given by the government or a commercial bank of an industrialized nation.
  - Loans have to be repaid at a later date and this can create severe problems for less-developed countries. Many loans have had to be renegotiated. Some less-developed nations have been forced to suspend interest payments for certain periods. There is always the danger that some nations will be forced to default on their foreign debts. In the most extreme cases, interest payments on foreign debts eat up a large proportion of the state's disposable income.

- **trade aid**
  - The industrialized nation reduces or eliminates tariffs to enable the less-developed country to have easier access for its export products. This enables the less-developed country to earn funds to pay for its development.
  - Perhaps the most beneficial type of aid. Being promoted by WTO.

- **cultural and technical aid**
  - Industrialized nations provide information and personnel to disseminate knowledge and teach skills.
  - Students from less-developed nations receive higher education in colleges and universities of developed countries. (Unfortunately, some prefer to remain rather than return to their own country where their expertise is greatly needed.)

- **military aid**
  - The major powers sell armaments to less-developed countries who need them because they feel threatened by neighbours or for internal security purposes. These expenditures and the cost of maintaining military forces can be a big drain on the limited budget of a less-developed nation.
  - Good way for industrial powers to sell off obsolete military hardware and keep the armaments industry in production. Sales of military equipment bring in large amounts of revenue for some industrialized nations.

Generally, all of these types of aid are available to less-developed countries through **bilateral** or **multilateral** aid agreements.

- *Multilateral aid* is available through international, non-governmental organizations. These organizations receive contributions from donor countries who are members. Control over disbursement of funds is in the hands of the agency. Member countries often contribute funds in accordance to the strength of their own economy; thus, the United States tends to have a dominant influence over the policies of organizations.

- Some important international organizations are:

OECD	Organization for Economic Cooperation and Development
IMF	International Monetary Fund. Helps countries in financial difficulty. Sets controls and conditions before approving loans.
World Bank	Makes direct loans to governments and provides technical assistance. Controlled by richer countries.
WHO	World Health Organization
FAO	Food and Agriculture Organization
UNICEF	United Nations Children's Fund

- Canada contributes to these funds. The United Nations objective is that each country should contribute 0.7% of its GDP to foreign aid. Few countries achieve this.

- *Bilateral aid* is available to the recipient country directly via the government of the assisting country. The assisting country maintains control over many of the decisions regarding the disposal of the funds.
- **CIDA** (*Canadian International Development Agency*) is responsible for the operation and administration of Canada's aid program. It provides technical, economic, and food aid.

Trade with less-developed countries

For less-developed countries the ability to earn income by exporting products to industrialized nations is an important objective. More can be earned through trade than through aid, and the extra income can be used to create more economic development. The problem is for the less-developed countries to have something to trade with the industrialized world. They have:

- **human resources**
  - They have an abundance of manpower, but it is rarely well educated or highly skilled.
  - This large pool of labour can be used to manufacture labour-intensive products. *e.g. clothes, toys, electronic goods.*
  - Wages are very low compared to what has to be paid in industrialized countries, but these low wages do not permit the workers to break out of the production-consumption cycle. They leave little surplus income that can be saved, invested, or even spent on consumer goods.

- **primary products**
  - Many less-developed nations rely heavily on the export of natural resources to pay for imports of manufactured goods from the industrialized countries.
  - They export primary products such as minerals, oil, forest products, sugar, coffee, tea, fruit, nuts, cacao, etc.. These resources are exported in a raw or semi-finished state. World prices for these primary products tend to fluctuate and are often low.
  - Foreign-owned multinationals are often in control of operations. To keep a docile and low-paid labour force these companies sometimes help to maintain an undemocratic form of government in place.

BILATERAL AID
Assisting country

MUTILATERAL AID
Industrialized contributing countries

International non-governmental organization

APPLICATION

1. What types of aid would be most appropriate in each of the following circumstances?

   a) Drought has reduced the rice crop in Bangladesh by two-thirds.

   _____

   b) A less-developed country wishes to establish an institute for research into animal diseases.

   _____

   c) A less-developed country wishes to export more leather goods to Canada.

   _____

   d) A Caribbean country wishes to build an airport to encourage more tourists from Canada.

   _____

   e) An African country must double its annual corn harvest if it is to feed its growing population in the future.

   _____

2. Discuss whether Canada should make a substantial increase in its foreign aid payments.

   a) How should the aid be disbursed?

   _____

   _____

   b) Should certain countries get preferential treatment?

   _____

   _____

3. How does Québec provide aid to less-developed countries? Consider the contributions made by:

   a) individuals

   _____

   _____

   b) business organizations

   _____

   _____

   c) government organizations

   _____

   _____

4. Interpret the flow chart below. How would you explain its meaning to some friends?

_____

_____

_____

_____

_____

_____

```
        ┌─────────────────┐
        │  Income spent   │
        │  on necessary   │
        │  consumption    │
        └─────────────────┘

        ┌─────────────────┐
        │Children have to │
        │work. Few schools│
        └─────────────────┘

        ┌─────────────────┐
        │  Poor diet and  │
        │   sanitation    │
        └─────────────────┘

┌──────────────┐   ┌──────┐   ┌──────────────┐   ┌─────────────────┐
│   POVERTY    │   │ Poor │   │Low literacy  │   │Resources used to│
└──────────────┘   │health│   │rate. Few     │   │produce consumer │
                   └──────┘   │technical     │   │necessities.     │
┌──────────────┐              │skills.       │   │Little left to   │
│Low per capita│              └──────────────┘   │invest and       │
│production of │                                 │develop new      │
│goods and     │   ┌──────────────┐              │capital goods.   │
│services      │   │Low productivity│            └─────────────────┘
└──────────────┘   └──────────────┘

               ┌──────────────┐
               │ Undeveloped  │
               │  technology  │
               └──────────────┘

               ┌──────────────┐
               │ Scarcity of  │
               │investment    │
               │  capital     │
               └──────────────┘

               ┌──────────────┐
               │Poorly        │
               │developed     │
               │resources     │
               └──────────────┘
```

Proposed changes for the international economic system

OUTLINE

There is an increasing gulf between the economic development of the less-developed countries and that of the industrialized nations. Increasingly, it is seen as a **North - South confrontation** which could eventually lead to conflict. Three-quarters of the world's population are responsible for only 21% of its total production. The remaining quarter enjoys the benefits of most of the production, has a much higher standard of living, better health, more leisure. The gap is constantly widening - the have-nots get more numerous and become hungrier each day.

There have been numerous international conferences to discuss the problems. Many less-developed countries formed the non-aligned group of nations. In an attempt to help the less-developed nations the following proposals have been put forward:

- **Stabilize prices**
  - The prices of primary products fluctuate and are often low. Prices tend to be controlled by demand from developed countries.
  - A large drop in the price for a primary product greatly reduces the income of a country which depends upon one or two main exports. World prices for copper, sugar, cotton tend to be low.
  - If the base price of these primary products could be stabilized, then the less-developed countries could undertake more effective economic planning because their main source of revenue would be assured. Long-term planning and growth would be more realistic.

- **Tariff reduction**
  - Industrialized countries often use high tariffs and quotas to protect home industries and limit competition from cheaper products coming from less-developed countries. Developing countries would benefit greatly if their products were not shut out by protectionist barriers. Inflation and high unemployment pressure governments to maintain these barriers. The World Trade Organization (WTO) is designed to reduce barriers to international trade, especially those between developed and developing nations.

- **Concentrate on food production**
  - In some less-developed countries large areas of land are devoted to producing cash crops for the export market. Some experts believe it would be more beneficial to hand these lands to the people to farm to produce food for themselves *(subsistence agriculture)*. Money saved on importing food would outweigh the money lost on exporting primary products.

- **Lower the birth rate**
  - This would make it possible to devote more funds to economic development while reducing the problem of over-population over a period of time.

- **Industrialize the less-developed nations**
  - These nations need to diversify their economy. Manufacturing will add value to local products before they are exported. It will provide more employment and reduce dependence on imports of foreign manufactured goods.

APPLICATION

1. The Québec economy is affected by changes in the world price of wood pulp, newsprint, copper, and aluminum.

    a) Does this mean that the province of Québec is similar to a less-developed country? Explain your response.

    _____

    _____

    b) Would Québec benefit from stabilized prices for these primary products?

    _____

    _____

2. Sudden price changes in the price of a basic commodity such as oil can spell crisis for less-developed countries. The price of oil climbed from $US 2.50 in 1970 to $US 35.00 in 1981 before falling back to about $US 13.00 a barrel in March 1998. In 2004 crude oil prices were rising past the $US 30.00 level again.

    a) Describe the probable effects of a rapid increase on the balance of payments of a LEDC country with no oil deposits.

    _____

    _____

    b) Describe the effects of a big increase on the balance of payments of a country with large oil deposits.

    _____

    _____

    c) Describe the outcome of a sudden drop in prices after a period of high prices on the economy of an oil-rich nation.

    _____

    _____

3. Industrialized countries are now scrambling to make efficient use of modern "high technology". Developing nations often lack the capital and technical resources necessary to introduce expensive modern techniques.

    What is likely to happen to the gap between industrialized and less-developed nations as more and more high technology is used?

    _____

    _____

    _____

    _____

    _____

    _____

Collectivist economies

OUTLINE

In the first module a distinction was made between **command economies** and **market economies**. In a command economy there is centralized control and decision-making. In contrast, many individual producers and consumers make decisions in a market economy. There are, however, no pure examples of such economic systems.

In times past communist countries such as the former Soviet Union, the former East Germany, Poland, Hungary, and Czechoslovakia <u>had</u> economic systems which most closely resembled command economies. In 2004, China, still had a communist government, but it was changing rapidly towards a more mixed market economy. North Korea is a last bastion of a command economy with disastrous consequences for the people. Cuba has a communist government, but its economy is held back by continuing US sanctions on trade with Cuba. Most other countries which retain a communist government are changing towards a market economy. Communists believe that the interests of the total population (or the **collective good**) are best served by an economic system with a large degree of government control. Such systems are referred to as **collectivist economies**.

Socialism originated as a reaction to the abuses of the Industrial Revolution. While workers toiled up to 16 hours a day for very low wages, some unscrupulous owners grew very wealthy. Some believed that an ideal society could be reorganized through public ownership and state planning. Robert Owen, a British factory owner and philanthropist, coined the word *socialism* for this philosophy.

Karl Marx was an important thinker in this movement to prevent exploitation of workers. In his *Communist Manifesto* Marx argued for the overthrow of the owners so that workers alone would share in the profits of their labours. Marx's ideas have influenced several forms of modern socialism. Three forms of modern socialism are:

      Marxism-Leninism (Communism)

      Social Democracy

      Third World socialism

They all believe that some degree of state control of the economic system is necessary to solve the problems of production and the equitable distribution of wealth.

Communist countries

(Few examples remain. The following characteristics applied to countries when they had a communist government.)

- The state took over most private property. It owned the land, the resources, the factories, the distribution system, and the housing.
- A powerful oligarchy belonging to the party in power exercised a strong central control over the economic system. This required detailed advance planning. Five year plans set production targets.
- Local managers and workers decided how to meet their assigned quota *(the amount the planners expect them to produce)*. There was little room for individual or local initiative.
- Because the plans were extremely complex there were mix-ups and shortages of materials that created problems. Productivity and quality tended to be variable. Productivity on collective farms and state farms was low so food shortages were common.
- The state also set prices and wages which were usually low in comparison to those in western countries. There was little inflation in the prices controlled by the state. Almost everyone had a job although some were under-employed.
- Priority was given to producing capital goods *(factories, dams, mines, transportation systems)* at the expense of luxury items for consumers.
- State control and central planning helped some countries, especially China, to improve their backward economies rapidly. Living standards were lower than in western countries.
- Farm workers produced large amounts of food on small plots of land allocated to each family. These privately operated plots were productive because farmers could make individual decisions about what to produce and they were allowed to sell their surplus at local markets. (In China this relaxation of controls now extends to entrepreneurial families in the cities too. Entrepreneurs are allowed to make goods and sell them on the free market. Their motivation and productivity are high. Foreign investors are using low-cost Chinese labour to produce consumer goods for the world market. China now has one of the world's fastest growing economies.)

Social democratic countries

- Some systems try to blend the ideas of socialism and democracy. Countries in western Europe have experimented with social democracy especially since the end of World War II (1945). Sweden, Norway, and Denmark are good examples, but the United Kingdom, the Netherlands, Germany, France, and Italy also have many social-democratic institutions, as does Canada.
- The ruling government party has been democratically elected in each of these countries.
- Private ownership still plays an essential role in the economy but the state assures certain services and regulates the economy for the collective good. Education and medical care are free. Railways and airlines were owned and operated by the state. Some key industries were also state owned.
- Troubled industries such as the manufacture of aircraft or automobiles were taken over by the state to keep them operating and reduce unemployment.
- Social democrats are often favourably disposed towards unions so wages and working conditions are reasonable.
- All this government involvement in the economy is expensive so high taxes are necessary to pay for all the services, regulations and policies. High taxes are a disincentive for some workers. However, the opportunity to buy homes, consumer goods, and leisure activities is sufficient incentive to make most people want to work productively.

(In recent years there has been a trend towards **privatization** *in many of these countries as more conservative governments sell state-owned industries to the private sector. The trend is towards less government control of the economy, balanced budgets, and lower levels of taxation. Inefficient businesses are forced to change or close while excess workers are retired or dismissed. The outcome has been lower rates of unemployment, greater productivity, and a more prosperous economy.)*

Third World countries

- Third World socialism has been adopted by many less-developed nations. Many were once colonies and their economies lag behind those of developed western nations.
- With a desire to improve their economic system quickly, less-developed countries leaned towards socialist ideas. To expand the economy and to eliminate the exploitation of the workers they control private ownership, especially foreign ownership.
- Large estates were broken up and redistributed among landless peasants.
- Dams, roads, railways, factories, schools, hospitals, and homes are constructed by the state.
- A major problem is the lack of adequate capital resources to finance all this development. Most less-developed countries need large loans and foreign aid to carry out their plans.
- Dictators who rob the economy to fill their own bank accounts are a scourge in some countries.

UPDATE

Because government control and centralized planning are now being relaxed by the governments of countries which formerly had collectivist economies, this outline may need to be updated. Make a note of recent changes in the space below. Indicate where the changes are occurring

Mixed economies

OUTLINE

In a pure **market economy** *free enterprise* would operate the economic system with no government involvement. **Capitalism** would have complete freedom to operate the economy. *Entrepreneurs* would decide what to produce and the available supply and consumer demand would determine prices. Through changes in their demands consumers would regulate the economy. The government would exercise no control.

In reality no pure market economies exist. In all societies some government participation in the economic system is deemed necessary. We use the term **mixed economy** when the government plays an important role even though the economy is based largely on free enterprise and the theory of capitalism. The government owns some of the resources and regulates some aspects of the economy.

- Entrepreneurs are fairly free to invest their capital as they wish. There are some government regulations to reduce the worst kinds of exploitation.
- If they invest wisely, entrepreneurs make considerable profits and build up important enterprises. On the other hand, some enterprises fail and workers have to be laid off.
- There are greater contrasts between the richer and poorer members of the society.
- Because government intervenes less, taxation rates can be lower.
- Despite its greater inequalities and lower economic security, the capitalist system tends to produce a higher standard of living for most people.

Free enterprise seems unable to cope with some economic problems:
- The tendency for giant multinational enterprises to control segments of the market has to be regulated by governments. Antitrust and anticartel legislation is being used to control the power of some multinationals (e.g the break up of Microsoft in the USA). The proposed MAI (Multilateral Agreement on Investments) is also aimed at monitoring this problem.
- Industrial pollution has to be subjected to government regulations and controls.
- Bitter disputes between labour and management require government arbitration.
- Unemployment and inflation rates need to be reduced by government policies.
- Workers displaced by rapidly changing technologies require state assistance.
- Long-term planning seems essential if the best use of natural resources, capital and labour is to be made.

Some people regard increased government planning and control as the best way to ensure future economic growth. Others are concerned that this reduces efficiency and slows down the economy.

The economic system of Canada including Québec

Canada has a mixed economy. Governments are more involved in the economy than they are in Japan or the United States.

- **Government of Canada**
  - Set up corporations such as Petro-Canada to have more influence in industry. Due to privatization of several crown corporations such as Canadian National Railways, Petro-Canada, Air Canada, the St Lawrence Seaway, and Canadair (now part of Bombardier), the Government of Canada now has only a few crown corporations such as Canada Post, the Canadian Broadcasting Corporation, Atomic Energy of Canada Ltd.
  - Canada Development Corporation was created to develop and maintain strong Canadian-controlled and managed corporations in the private sector of the economy. Its objective is to gain control in leading corporations. Investments have been made in petrochemicals, mining, oil and gas, health care and electronic word processing.
  - Controls the economy through legislation and regulations established by its many commissions
  - Keeps industries viable by giving large grants for research and modernization. These policies are being criticized by some economists.

- **Government of Québec**
    - Acquired control of certain companies such as Asbestos Corporation and Domtar to have more influence on the economy, but there is a trend to sell back some crown corporations to the private sector.
    - Assists manufacturers through the *Société de développement industriel (SDI)*. SDI cannot acquire a majority share in any company but it can effectively influence a company by its right to have one or more directors on the board of the company.
    - The *Caisse de dépôt et placement* invests the funds collected for the Québec Pension Plan and the civil servants' pension plans. It also invests funds from various government insurance schemes. Its investments are in the billions of dollars so it is one of the largest investors in both the province and other parts of Canada.
    - The government has other agencies which play a large part in the economy: e.g. *Hydro-Québec, Société des alcools, Loto-Québec.*

APPLICATION

1. Ascertain which type of economic system *(mixed, collectivist, or changing)* is found in each of the following countries.

Albania	_____	Kuwait	_____
Australia	_____	New Zealand	_____
Brazil	_____	Nicaragua	_____
China	_____	Taiwan	_____
Cuba	_____	South Korea	_____
Germany	_____	Sweden	_____
Singapore	_____	United Kingdom	_____
India	_____	United States	_____
Israel	_____	Russia	_____
Japan	_____	Mexico	_____

2. In the country of Laurentia the Ministry of Education introduced a new course in Economic Education for all Secondary 5 students. Each of the 125 000 students taking the course had to have a textbook. Outline what would happen:

a) if Laurentia had a collectivist economic system.

_____

_____

_____

b) if Laurentia had a mixed economic system which included several privately owned publishing firms.

_____

_____

_____

3. The degree of state involvement depends to a considerable extent on the political philosophy of the ruling party. Indeed, a change of the party in power usually results in some shift in the position of a country on the economic spectrum. A right-wing party favours capitalism and reductions in state control. Left-wing parties lean towards more government regulation and intervention.

    Where would you place each of the countries listed below on the economic spectrum diagram which follows?

    COUNTRIES:

Canada	China	Cuba	France	Japan	Sweden
Taiwan	U.K.	U.S.A.	Russia	Germany	North Korea

    LEFT   **RIGHT**

Socialism	**Mixed economy**	**Capitalism**
Regulation &		*Free*
public ownership		*enterprise*

    The economic spectrum

4. Where would you place each of the following governments on the spectrum according to their economic policies?

    a) The present government of Canada _____

    b) The previous government of Canada _____

    c) The present government of Québec _____

    d) The previous government of Québec _____

    e) The present government of the United States _____

    f) The present government of the United Kingdom _____

5. Consider the economic policies of our present federal and provincial governments.

    a) Do they tend to favour state intervention or the expansion of private enterprise? Give evidence to support your answer.

    _____

    _____

    _____

    b) What might happen if the main opposition party came to power?

    _____

    _____

6.　Complete the table below to compare and contrast collectivist and mixed economies.

	COLLECTIVIST ECONOMY	MIXED ECONOMY
Who decides WHAT will be produced?		
Who decides HOW it will be produced?		
What happens if the factory is not very productive?		
Who determines how to distribute goods and services?		
How are PRICES & WAGES determined?		

7.　Consider each of the following statements and decide if it describes a characteristic of a *mixed economy* or of a *collectivist economy.*

a) The state assures that everyone gets a fair share by fixing prices and wages rather than by having progressive income tax scales.　_____

b) The state is responsible for education and health services which are provided free of charge.　_____

c) Consumer demands determine what will be produced, in what quantity, and at what price.　_____

d) Unless they belong to the state, companies have to be profitable to be able to continue operations.　_____

e) Most companies belong to the private sector but the government does nationalize some key industries to help them to survive.　_____

f) Most businesses belong to the state but there are many small private entrepreneurs who are allowed to sell their surplus production.　_____

g) Decisions made by the central planners carry more weight than initiatives of local workers.　_____

h) Economic activity is based on free competition in the market place and the government intervenes only if consumers need some help.　_____

Glossary

absolute advantage—a condition which exists when a nation can produce a good more efficiently

advertising—messages designed to encourage people to buy a specific product or behave in a certain way

affiliation—the official association of a union local or a union organization with a larger labour body

appreciation—an increase in market value

arbitration—labour and management engaged in an industrial dispute agree to accept the decision of a third party, an arbitrator, whose decision is binding

autonomous—an independent, self-governing unit

balance of international payments—a summary of all financial transactions between Canadians and residents of the rest of the world over a period of one year

balance of trade—the difference between the money value of a country's merchandise exports and the value of its merchandise imports

Bank Act—legislation that regulates the lending activities of financial institutions in Canada

bank rate—the rate of interest which the Bank of Canada charges chartered banks when they borrow money

barter—trading one product for another without the use of money as a medium of exchange

bilateral agreement—an agreement negotiated between two countries to the exclusion of other countries

bilateral trade—trade between two countries

birth rate—the annual rate of births in a country expressed as the number of births per thousand

bond—a interest-bearing certificate issued by a company or a government

boycott—customers decide not to buy or use certain products

branch banking—a bank establishes a number of branches over a geographic area

break even point—point reached when revenues are equal to costs

budget—a plan for handling income and expenses

capital—money that has been saved which can be used to buy capital goods or to set up or operate a business

capital account—record of the net flow of capital between one country and the rest of the world

capital gain—if you sell something at a price higher than the one you paid, the difference is your capital gain

capital gains tax—direct tax on the profits made by the seller on the sale of either shares or property after a fixed limit has been surpassed

capital intensive industry—costs of equipment used are high in relation to labour costs

capital resources (goods)—the machinery, equipment, tools, and buildings used to produce goods and services

caveat emptor—Latin for "let the buyer beware". You buy at your own risk.

centrale—a Québec term referring to an association or federation of many union locals, often in a related area

certification—process which ensures unions have met all the legal requirements to negotiate a collective agreement for their members

chairman—a person chosen by the shareholders to chair meetings of the directors of a company

charter—a document setting out the rights and obligations of a company

chartered banks—banks set up by permission of the federal government and which function under the regulation of the Bank Act

chequing account—bank account used for day-to-day transactions on which no interest is paid

collateral—something of value which serves as a pledge that credit payments will be made

collective agreement—a contract between a union and an employer

command economy—an economic system where decision-making and control of production are centralized in the hands of the government

comparative advantage—a condition that exists when a country enjoys an absolute advantage in the production of two or more products, but has a relatively greater advantage in the production of one of those goods

conciliation—a process during negotiations in which a third-party, a conciliator, suggests ways of overcoming or compromising on the problems

conditional sales contract—a contract issued by a finance company that sets down the terms of the loan and its repayment

confederation—in the case of caisses populaires, it is an alliance of federations to offer better services

conglomerate—an integrated group of companies operating in several distinct markets

consumer—a person who buys goods and services

consumer loan company—a company established to make loans to the public usually without collateral

CPI / Consumer Price Index—is a statistical tool used to measure the percentage change over time in the cost of a standard set of goods and services

contract—an agreement between two parties. It may be oral but must be written to be legally binding.

cooperative—a business organized more for the benefit of its shareholders rather than to make a high profit

corporation—a company with a charter which permits it to own property, buy and sell goods, make products as if it were a single legal person

credit—the ability to buy now and to pay later

credit limit—the maximum amount a person is allowed to buy on credit. It varies from person to person.

credit manager—one who gives credit at a financial institution or retail store

creditor—a person or organization to whom one owes money

crown corporation—a company owned by the government which enjoys some autonomy

current account—a record of the net flow of goods and services between one country and the rest of the world

demand—the quantity of a good or service that consumers are willing to buy at a given price

deposit money—money deposited in banks that one may withdraw or write cheques on

depreciation—a decrease in market value

depression—the lowest point in the business cycle where production is low and unemployment is high

devaluation—a reduction in the value of a currency by its government in terms of other currencies

direct tax—tax paid directly by the person or firm on whom it is levied

dividend—that part of a company's profits which is distributed among the shareholders

economic organization—the way society organizes its resources to produce goods and services

employed—those who are at work, or who are not at work because of illness, vacation, strike, or other

entrepreneur—a person who takes the risk offsetting up and organizing a business which he/she hopes will be profitable

estate—personal property of an individual left at the time of death

exchange control—government controls regulating purchases of foreign currencies with domestic currency

exchange rate—the price of one currency in terms of another

excise duty—indirect tax levied on imported luxury goods

excise tax—indirect tax on certain goods produced domestically which are considered luxuries

exploitation—the act of utilizing the labour or energy and resources of a person or region without giving just or equivalent return

export—to ship merchandise abroad to foreign countries

face amount—cash payment made on the maturity of an insurance policy

factors of production—things needed to produce goods and services: natural, human, and capital resources

financial institution—a business organization dealing with money transactions e.g. bank

first world—the industrialized nations in the Western group

fiscal policy—the use of the budget by the government to regulate the economy

fixed costs—expenses incurred in operating a business which are continuous e.g. rent, taxes

fixed income—an income that does not change (often a pension)

floating exchange rate—a system in which exchange rates are determined day-to-day through the forces of supply and demand

foreign exchange—the currencies of other countries used to pay for imported goods, services, and investments

foreign exchange reserves—currencies and liquid assets held by a country that can be used to settle international debts

foreign investments—purchases by non-residents of business enterprises and other assets capable of yielding a return

fractional reserves—banks are only required to keep a fraction of their deposits as reserves against possible withdrawals

free trade—the policy of non-interference in the free flow of goods between countries

fringe benefits—non-wage benefits such as paid vacations, life insurance, pension, sickness plans

goods—tangible objects or articles produced to be used by consumers

government securities—bonds issued by the various levels of government

grievance—complaint by either union or management against the other party concerning an alleged injustice or misinterpretation of the collective agreement

GIC / Guaranteed Investment Certificate—an investment with a higher rate of interest than a savings account for people who accept to put away their money for a period of up to five years

gold standard—use of a fixed amount of gold as the basic standard of value of a currency

guarantee—an undertaking to repair or replace certain parts that do not meet the standards promised by the company

guarantor—a person who co-signs an application for credit to assure that payments will be made

horizontal integration—a series of companies in the same market which have been merged under one control

human resources—the people, especially those who are able to work to supply the physical and mental labour required to produce goods and services

IMF / International Monetary Fund—a fund that enables member countries to stabilize the exchange rate of their currency through short-term loans and special drawing rights

import—to receive merchandise from abroad

indirect tax—a tax not levied directly on the final consumer of a good or service but usually paid by the final consumer in the price of the good or service

industrial revolution—the substitution of machines for hard manual labour in the production of goods

inflation—a sharp increase in the general level of prices

installment buying—a procedure whereby the purchaser pays for a good over a period of time but receives the item at the outset of the transaction

insurance company—a financial institution grouping people who share risks e.g. life, accidents

interest—the cost of borrowing

investment—the purchase or production of real capital with savings made available through banks or "near banks"

job security—a clause in a collective agreement protecting a worker's job to some degree against changes in working conditions, new methods, etc.

labour force—that portion of the population, 15 years of age and over, that is employed or seeking work

labour intensive industry—costs of labour are high in relation to costs of materials and equipment

laissez-faire—a doctrine opposing governmental interference in economic affairs beyond the minimum necessary

legal tender—money

less-developed country—a nation with its economy still in a less-developed stage, usually short of investment capital and under-industrialized

liability—responsibility for debts. Unlimited liability = owner is responsible for all debts. Limited liability = shareholders can lose no more than the amount of their investment.

line of credit—a financial institution grants to a business or industrial firm the right to borrow up to a fixed amount

liquid securities—stock, bonds, and other forms of "near money" that may be easily turned into cash

loan—a sum of money borrowed for temporary use which must be repaid with interest

local union—the smallest unit in a federation of unions

lockout—the employer closes the doors to the work place in an attempt to intimidate the workers during negotiations

loss leader—a product that is sold for a low price to attract people to the store in the hope that they will purchase more goods

market—any place where buyers and sellers come together to exchange goods and services

market economy—an economic system which operates with a minimum of government control

marketing—activities to bring products to market, to make consumers aware of them

marketing board—a government agency set up to regulate the supply, sales, and prices of farm commodities e.g. eggs, milk, wheat

merger—one company acquires control of or buys up another

minimum wage—the lowest wage an employer may pay to a worker. It is set by law and varies from province to province.

mixed economy—an economic system where both private citizens and the government share in decision-making and production

mixed enterprise—a business partly owned by private interests and partly by the government

money supply—the total mass of money in circulation and demand deposits in financial institutions

moral suasion—the force of the opinion of others leading you to do what is considered right

mortgage—a loan obtained in order to purchase real estate

multilateral trade—the exchange of goods, services, and investments among all nations without interference

multilateral trade agreement—a trade agreement signed by several countries

multinational—a company which has branches in more than one country. Usually big and powerful.

natural resources—resources provided by nature

near bank—a financial institution that provides services similar to the chartered banks but cannot change the money supply in making loans e.g. caisses populaires, trust companies, credit unions

needs—things that people must have to survive – basic necessities

opportunity cost—the cost of an economic choice; what you do without when you choose to buy certain goods and/or services

partnership—a business with more than one owner and unlimited liability

per capita income—an indicator of the economic wealth of a country, obtained by dividing the GNP by the total population of the country

picketing—legal marching near the work place by union members to publicize a strike, encourage members' support, discourage scabs

policy—a life insurance contract that sets down the terms both parties agree to

premium—price paid for a life insurance policy

president—a paid employee hired by the directors of a company to be in charge of the day-to-day administration of the company

price—what the seller asks the buyer to pay for a good or service

primary activities—are based on the exploitation of natural resources e.g. farming, mining, fishing

principal—the amount of money borrowed

primary reserves—an amount specified in the Bank Act as the minimum percentage of all deposits that banks must hold as cash

prime rate—the rate of interest which banks charge their best customers i.e. large, stable corporate customers

productivity—measure of the productiveness of a person, team, or company. Total output.

profit—the difference between total revenues and total costs; what the business hopes to gain

progressive tax—the rate is automatically adjusted to the different capacities of the individual to pay

proportional tax—has a flat rate but its yield depends on the assessed value of the good

proprietorship—a business owned by one person with unlimited liability

protectionism—the policy of protecting a country's industries from foreign competition by imposing tariffs or quotas on foreign goods

public debt—is the outstanding debt of all levels of government usually financed through bonds

purchasing power—the quantity of goods and services that one can obtain with a given sum of money

quota—a specific limit on the amount of imports entering a country

real estate—immovable property such as a house or land

recession—is the period in the business cycle when production is slowing down and unemployment is increasing

RRSP / Registered Retirement Savings Plan—allows you to invest for your retirement and defer the income tax payable on the amount invested

regressive tax—the same rate is paid by everyone regardless of ability to pay

regulation—a restriction imposed by government authorities

repossession—taking back the goods bought on installment plans if payments are not made

retail vendor—one who sells goods or services directly to the customer

revaluation—an increase in the value of a currency by its government in terms of other currencies

right—brief option to buy a stock

savings—money which is not spent on current consumption and is put aside for the future

savings deposits—bank/trust company accounts for savings on which interest is paid to the depositor

scab—a person paid by management to take the job of a unionized worker while that worker is on a legal strike

secondary activities—are those which manufacture goods

secondary reserves—additional monies that banks may be required to keep in reserve at the direction of the Bank of Canada. The amount may range from 0 to 12% of the bank's total deposits.

second world—developed nations which formerly had a centralized communist economy

seniority—an employee's status relative to the other workers based on the period employed. Used to determine order for layoff, transfer, promotion, assignment, etc.

services—intangible actions performed for a fee to help or advise the consumer

share—a part in the ownership of a business which entitles its owner to a share in the dividends of the company

société d'état—French term for "crown corporation"

stagflation—a period when the economy is stagnant while unemployment and inflation are both high

standard of living—the living conditions of a consumer or a nation

strike—workers stop work as a means of exerting pressure on an employer to accept their terms

subsidiary—a company with over half its shares controlled by a parent company

subsidy—a government grant to support a business or public service

supply—the quantity of a good or service that is offered for sale at a given price

tariff—the duty levied on imported goods by a government

term insurance—life insurance taken out for a specific period of time

tertiary activities—provide services to consumers

the "North"—industrialized countries with relatively high per capita incomes and standards of living. Mostly found in N. America and Europe.

the "South"—under-developed countries of the Third World with low per capita incomes, high birth rates, inadequate economic development, etc. Mostly in Latin America, Africa, and Asia.

third world—less-developed nations

trade union—an organization of workers to improve their mutual working conditions, wages, etc.

traditional economy—an economic system where people rely mostly on natural resources and their own labour for subsistence

transfer payment—revenues collected by one level of government and given to another level to provide services equivalent to those in richer areas

treasury bills—short term government bonds sold by auction every Thursday

true savings account—a savings account with a higher rate of interest which does not allow chequing privileges

trust—property administered on behalf of an individual, usually by a trust company

trust company—a financial institution that manages property and money

unemployed—those without work but who are available and looking for work

unit banks—banks which do not have branches and operate locally

variable costs—change according to the volume of business, of changes in supply and demand

variable credit—sometimes called a "revolving charge account". It extends credit to a preset limit. A monthly minimum charge must be paid. Interest is charged on any unpaid balance

vertical integration—a group of companies which supply one another with goods or services needed to produce a line of goods

wants—things that people desire, would like to have, but they are not essential for survival

warranty—a promise that the product will meet certain standards

working age population—all people aged 15 and over

Statistical Tables

(Revised June 2004)

Canada: Gross Domestic Product

The GDP is a measure of all the final goods and services produced in Canada in one year. It is given in current dollars for each year. For easier comparison it is also given in constant 1992 dollars adjusted for inflation. (The current base year is 1997).

Figures are in millions of dollars.

Year	GDP (Current dollars)	Real GDP (Constant dollars)	Annual change %
1930	6 009	51 262	-3.3
1935	4 514	45 357	7.2
1940	6 987	63 722	13.3
1945	12 063	89 170	-2.4
1950	19 125	104 821	7.8
1955	29 250	134 889	9.5
1960	39 448	164 126	2.9
1965	58 050	281 249	6.5
1970	90 367	351 434	2.6
1971	98 630	370 859	5.5
1972	110 124	390 702	5.4
1973	129 196	418 797	7.2
1974	154 290	436 151	4.1
1975	173 893	445 813	2.2
1976	200 296	470 291	5.5
1977	221 358	486 562	3.5
1978	245 526	506 413	4.1
1979	280 309	527 703	4.2
1980	315 245	535 007	1.4
1981	360 494	551 305	3.0
1982	379 734	535 113	-2.9
1983	411 160	549 843	2.8
1984	449 249	581 038	5.7
1985	485 139	612 416	5.4
1986	511 796	628 575	2.6
1987	558 106	654 360	4.1
1988	611 785	686 176	4.9
1989	656 190	703 577	2.5
1990	678 135	705 464	0.3
1991	683 239	692 247	-1.9
1992	698 544	698 544	0.9
1993	724 960	714 583	2.3
1994	767 506	748 350	4.7
1995	807 088	769 082	2.8
1996	833 921	782 130	1.7
1997	873 947	813 031	3.9
1998	985 704	838 265	3.1
1999	976 716	898 500	4.7

Source: Statistics Canada

GDPs of selected countries

Figures are the lastest available in 2003. (In most cases figures are estimates for 2002).

All dollar amounts are given in US dollars.
n.a. = not available

COUNTRY	GDP billions of US $	GDP PER CAPITA US $	REAL GROWTH RATE %	INFLATION RATE %
Argentina	391	10 200	-14.7	-1.1
Australia	582	27 000	3.6	4.4
Bangladesh	203	1 570	5.3	1.4
Brazil	1 340	7 400	1.9	6.9
Canada	923	29 400	3.4	2.6
Chile	153	10 000	3.1	3.6
China	6 000	4 600	8.0	0.3
Cuba	26	2 300	0.0	0.3
Egypt	258	3 700	2.5	2.3
Ethiopia	46	700	7.3	-11.2
France	1 540	25 700	1.1	1.6
Germany	2 184	26 600	0.4	2.5
Greece	201	19 000	3.5	3.4
Haiti	12	1 700	-1.2	14.2
India	2 660	2 540	4.3	3.7
Indonesia	687	3 000	3.3	11.5
Iran	456	7 000	5.0	11.3
Ireland	111	28 500	3.9	4.9
Israel	122	19 000	-1.1	1.1
Italy	1 438	25 000	0.4	2.8
Jamaica	10	3 700	1.1	7.0
Japan	3 550	28 000	-0.3	-0.7
North Korea	22	1 000	1.0	n.a.
South Korea	931	19 400	5.8	4.3
Mexico	920	9 000	-0.3	6.4
Netherlands	434	26 900	0.3	4.5
New Zealand	75	19 500	3.1	2.6
Nicaragua	12	2 500	2.5	11.0
Nigeria	106	840	3.5	16.5
Norway	143	31 800	1.6	3.0
Pakistan	299	2 100	3.3	3.1
Peru	132	4 800	-0.3	2.0
Philippines	335	4 000	2.8	6.1
Poland	368	9 500	1.2	5.5
Portugal	182	18 000	0.8	4.4
Russia	1 270	8 800	4.0	21.5
Saudi Arabia	241	10 600	1.6	-0.5
Singapore	106	24 700	-2.2	1.0
Somalia	4	550	3.0	over 100
Spain	828	20 700	2.0	3.6
Sweden	227	25 400	1.8	2.4
Switzerland	231	31 700	2.0	1.0
Taiwan	386	17 200	-2.2	1.3
U.K. (Britain)	1 520	25 300	1.6	1.8
United States	10 082	36 300	2.5	1.6
Vietnam	168	2 100	4.7	-0.4

Source: Canadian Global Almanac 2004

Canada: Gross Domestic Product (1997-2003)

Expenditure-based GDP at market prices in constant 1997 dollars

	$ millions
1997	882 734
1999	969 750
2000	1 020 786
2001	1 040 388
2002	1 074 516
2003	1 092 891
2004	
2005	
2006	
2007	

Source: Statistics Canada

Canada's real GDP at market prices

in chained 1997 dollars

Source: Statistics Canada

The 25 largest corporations in Canada (2003)

By sales as of 2003 12 31
Revenue and assets are given in millions of $CAN

	CORPORATION	REVENUE	ASSETS	EMPLOYEES
1	General Motors Corp of Canada Ltd	36 514	—	—
2	George Weston Ltd	29 198	17 338	145 000
3	Royal Bank of Canada (RBC)	24 829	403 033	60 812
4	Sun Life Financial	22 056	109 209	14 905
5	Magna International Inc	21 506	12 726	74 000
6	Bombardier Inc	21 321	25 569	75 000
7	Ford of Canada Ltd	20 831	10 219	15 723
8	Alcan Inc	19 092	41 413	50 000
9	BCE *(Bell)*	19 056	39 331	64 000
10	Imperial Oil Ltd	17 840	12 361	6 256
11	Bank of Nova Scotia	17 261	285 892	43 986
12	Canadian Imperial Bank of Commerce (CIBC)	17 122	277 147	36 630
13	Onex Corporation	17 108	14 621	102 000
14	DaimlerChrysler of Canada Ltd	16 939	—	—
15	Manulife Financial	16 656	77 516	13 000
16	Power Corporation of Canada	15 747	107 723	28 000
17	Toronto-Dominion Bank	15 626	273 532	41 934
18	EnCana Corporation *(Oil & gas)*	14 316	31 157	3 854
19	Honda Canada Inc	14 000	—	4 800
20	Nortel Networks Ltd	13 745	20 704	—
21	Bank of Montreal (BOM)	13 147	256 494	33 912
22	Hydro-Quebec	13 002	59 078	20 972
23	Petro-Canada	12 209	14 590	4 514
24	Quebecor Inc	11 222	15 115	50 000
25	The Thompson Corp	10 660	24 219	43 000

Source: Financial Post June 2004

The world's largest businesses (2003)

By sales as of 2002 12 31

			$US billions
1	Exxon Mobil	USA	210.4
2	Wal-Mart Stores	USA	193.3
3	General Motors	USA	184.7
4	Ford Motor	USA	180.6
5	DaimlerChrysler	USA	150.1
6	Shell Group	UK/Netherlands	149.1
7	BP	UK	148.1
8	General Electric	USA	129.9
9	Mitsubishi	Japan	126.6
10	Toyota Motor	Japan	121.4
11	Mitsui	Japan	118.0
12	Citigroup	USA	111.8
13	Itochu	Japan	109.8
14	Total Fina Elf	France	105.9
15	Nippon Telephone	Japan	103.2
16	Enron	USA	100.8
17	AXA	France	92.8
18	Sumitomo	Japan	91.8
19	IBM	USA	88.4
20	Marubeni	Japan	85.4
21	Volkswagen	Germany	78.9
22	Hitachi	Japan	76.1
23	Siemens	Germany	74.9
24	ING Group	Netherlands	71.2
25	Allianz	Germany	71.0

Source: The Economist World of Figures 2003

Large companies in Quebec (2003)

Revenue is given in millions of $CAN

#	Company	Revenue
1	Royal Bank of Canada	24 829
2	Bombardier Inc	21 321
3	Alcan Inc	19 092
4	BCE	19 056
5	Power Corporation of Canada	15 747
6	Bank of Montreal	13 147
7	Hydro-Quebec	13 002
8	Quebecor Inc	11 222
9	Air Canada	8 368
10	Mouvement des caisses Desjardins	7 712
11	Ultramar Ltd	6 040
12	Canadian National	5 884
13	METRO Inc	5 567
14	McKesson Corporation Canada	5 400
15	Abitibi-Consolidated Inc	4 786
16	Domtar Inc	4 777
17	National Bank of Canada	4 665
18	Le Groupe Jean Coutu (PJC) Inc	4 052
19	Caisse de dépôt et placement du Québec	3 662
20	Cascades Inc	3 450
21	Saputo Inc	3 398
22	Alimentation Couche-Tard Inc	3 374
23	L'Industrielle-Alliance	3 352
24	Groupe SNC-Lavalin Inc	3 265
25	Tembec Inc	2 873
26	Loto-Québec	2 779

Source: Financial Post June 2004

Large foreign-owned companies in Canada (2003)

Company		Foreign capital
General Motors of Canada Ltd	USA	100%
Ford of Canada Ltd	USA	100%
Imperial Oil Ltd	USA	70%
DaimlerChrysler Canada Ltd	USA	100%
Honda Canada Ltd	Japan	100%
Shell Canada Ltd	Netherlands	78%
Costco Wholesale Corp.	USA	100%
Telus Corporation	USA	30%
Sears Canada Inc	USA	55%
Ultramar Ltd	USA	100%
Canada Safeway Ltd	USA	100%
IBM Canada Ltd	USA	100%
A&P Supermarkets	USA	100%
Toyota Canada Inc	Japan	100%
Cargill Ltd	USA	100%
ING Canada Inc	Netherlands	100%
Aviva Canada Inc	USA	100%

Source: Financial Post June 2004

Canada's top Crown Corporations (2003)

Revenue figures are in millions of $CAN

#	Company	Revenue	Employees
1	Hydro-Québec	13 002	20 972
2	Canada Post	6 154	65 767
3	Ontario Lotteries	5 762	7 941
4	Ontario Power Generation Inc	5 178	13 000
5	British Columbia Hydro & Power	4 407	6 013
6	Hydro One Inc *(Toronto)*	4 058	3 967
7	Caisse de dépôt et placement du Québec	3 662	2 500
8	Canadian Wheat Board	3 340	500
9	Insurance Corp of B. C.	3 189	—
10	Alberta Liquor Commision	3 152	
11	Ontario Liquor Board	3 119	6 754
12	Loto-Québec	2 779	6 800
13	EPCOR Utilities Inc *(Edmonton)*	2 589	2 300
14	Toronto Hydro Corporation	2 499	1 699
15	Canada Mortgage and Housing Corporation	2 361	1 799
16	Workplace Safety & Insurance Board	2 243	4 513
17	Bank of Canada	1 972	—
18	Société des alcools du Québec	1 874	6 124
19	Manitoba Hydroelectricity Board	1 869	5 365
20	B. C. Liquor Distribution	1 830	—

Source: Financial Post June 2004

Largest US corporations (2003)

US$ millions

#	Company		
1	Wal-Mart Stores	General merchandise	258 681
2	Exxon Mobil	Oil refining	213 199
3	General Motors	Motor vehicles	195 645
4	Ford Motor	Motor vehicles	164 496
5	General Electric	Diversified financial	134 187
6	ChevronTexaco	Oil refining	112 937
7	ConocoPhillips	Oil refining	99 468
8	Citigroup	Banking	94 713
9	IBM	Office equipment	89 131
10	American Int'l Group	Insurance	81 300
11	Hewlett-Packard	Office equipment	73 061
12	Verizon Communications	Telecommunications	67 752
13	Home Depot	Specialty retailer	64 816
14	Berkshire Hathaway	Insurance	63 859
15	Altria Group	Tobacco	60 704
16	McKeeson	Health care	57 129
17	Cardinal Health	Health care	56 830
18	State Farm Insurance Cos	Insurance	56 065
19	Kroger	Food & drug	53 791
20	Fannie Mae	Diversified financial	53 767
21	Boeing	Aerospace	50 485
22	Amerisourcebergen	Health care	49 657
23	Target	General merchandise	48 163
24	Bank of America Corp.	Banking	48 065
25	Pfizer	Pharmaceuticals	47 950

Source: Fortune 500 (2004 04 05)

Labour force: sectors of activity

Figures are percentages

YEAR	PRIMARY SECTOR	SECONDARY SECTOR	TERTIARY SECTOR
1951	18.4	38.4	43.2
1961	11.6	43.2	54.2
1971	10.2	31.7	57.2
1981	6.8	25.4	67.2
1991	5.5	21.3	72.7
2001	6.0	20.0	74.0

Unemployment rates among graduates

Figures are percentages

(Canada 2003)

Post-secondary diploma	5.9%
University degree	5.5%
Bachelor's degree	5.7%
Above bachelor's degree	5.0%

(Quebec 2001)

Vocational diploma	12.3%
CEGEP pre-university	10.5%
CEGEP technical	5.4%
University -Bachelor's degree	4.0%
University -Master's degree	3.7%
University -Doctorate	6.2%

Source: The Gazette (2004 02 21)

Labour force: unemployment rates

Figures are percentages of the labour force

	1970	1980	1990	1992	2002
Canada	5.7	7.5	8.1	11.3	7.5
Québec	7.0	9.8	10.1	12.8	8.5
Ontario	4.4	6.8	6.3	10.8	7.0
Man.	5.3	5.5	7.2	9.7	4.9
Sask.	4.2	4.4	7.0	8.2	5.0
Alberta	5.1	3.7	7.0	9.5	4.9
B.C.	7.7	6.8	8.3	10.5	8.4
Nfld.	7.3	13.3	17.1	20.2	18.5
N.S.	5.3	9.7	10.5	13.2	7.4
N.B.	6.3	11.0	12.1	12.8	10.3
P.E.I.	n.a.	10.6	14.9	17.9	10.9

Source: Statistics Canada

Quebec: Sectors of employment
(March 2004)

Agriculture	52 600
Mining, fishing, forestry, trapping	32 100
Public services	32 700
Construction	147 400
Manufacturing	620 400
Commerce	590 000
Transportation, warehousing	172 500
Finance, insurance, real estate	197 200
Professional services, science, technology	224 200
Business management, administration	103 400
Educational services	259 100
Health services and welfare	453 800
Information, culture, recreation	155 600
Hotels and restaurants	204 700
Other services	159 100
Public administration	210 600

Source: La Presse (2004 05 05)

Labour force: Canada and Québec
(2002)

Figures are in thousands.

	Population over 14 years	Labour force	Participation rate	Employed	Employment rate	Unemployed	Unemployment rate
Canada	23 994	16 925	67.5%	15 650	62.4%	1 276	7.5%
Québec	6 055	3 992	65.9%	3 654	60.3%	338	8.5%

Source: Statistics Canada

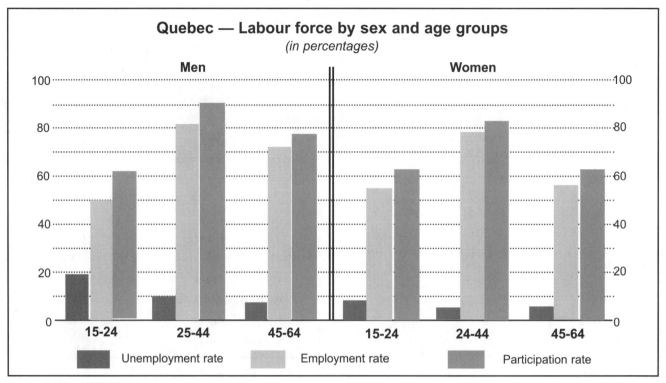

Quebec — Labour force by sex and age groups
(in percentages)

Men | **Women**

Legend: Unemployment rate | Employment rate | Participation rate

Source: La Presse (2004 05 05)

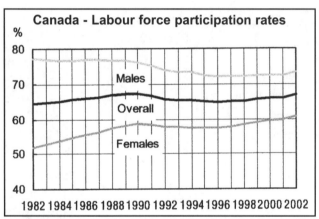

Canada - Labour force participation rates

Source: Statistics Canada

Canada: Population aged 15-19 years (1921-1991)

Source: Statistics Canada

Increases in mean annual salary by decades (1920-1990)

Decade	Increase in mean salary over the decade
1920-1930	12%
1930-1940	10%
1940-1950	34%
1950-1960	43%
1960-1970	37%
1970-1980	9%
1980-1990	2%

Source: La Presse (1994 03 30)

Comparison of men's and women's mean salaries (1920-1990)
Salaries are quoted in dollars

	Mean salary for men	Mean salary for women
1920	7 500	4 100
1930	8 300	5 000
1940	9 600	4 700
1950	12 800	7 400
1960	18 000	10 000
1970	26 200	13 700
1980	29 900	15 700
1990	29 800	17 900

Source: La Presse (1994 03 30)

One and two-earner families (1967-1991)

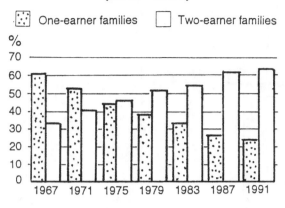

Source: La Presse (1994 03 17)

Average weekly earnings
in dollars

	2001	2002
Mining and oil extraction	1 153.12	1 167.98
Construction	800.80	804.22
Manufacturing	808.10	830.14
Transportation	741.65	764.40
Finance and insurance	852.32	852.78
Real estate	611.35	609.79
Professional, scientific, technical	885.14	900.02
Educational services	694.30	725.27
Health care and social assistance	581.36	605.12
Accommodation and food services	286.00	292.02
Public administration	791.95	833.52

Source: Statistics Canada

Level of consumption according to the educational level of the head of the household

Highest educational level achieved	Percentage of consumers whose level of consumption is			
	Very low	Low	High	Very high
Elementary	46.8	29.2	16.3	7.7
Secondary	18.8	25.8	29.9	25.5
College	5.7	19.6	29.6	45.1
University	7.1	14.1	20.9	57.9

Source: Office de la Protection du consommateur

Level of consumption according to age

Age group	Percentage of consumers whose level of consumption is			
	Very low	Low	High	Very high
18 - 35 years	13.3	22.6	33.8	30.3
36 - 54 years	18.9	25.9	24.8	30.4
55 and over	48.0	26.7	14.5	10.8

Source: Office de la Protection du consommateur

Average household expenditure (2001)

	Average expenditure $	Share of budget %
Total expenditure	**57 742**	**100.0**
Personal taxes	12 218	21.2
Shelter	10 984	19.0
Transportation	7 596	13.2
Food	6 438	11.1
Recreation	3 453	6.0
Insurance & pension payments	3 125	5.4
Household operation	2 619	4.5
Clothing	2 398	4.2
Household furnishing & equipment	1 655	2.9
Health care	1 420	2.5
Gifts and contributions	1 259	2.2
Tobacco & alcoholic beverages	1 313	2.3
Education	898	1.6
Personal care	960	1.7
Reading materials	276	0.5
Games of chance	267	0.5
Miscellaneous	865	1.5

Source: Statistics Canada

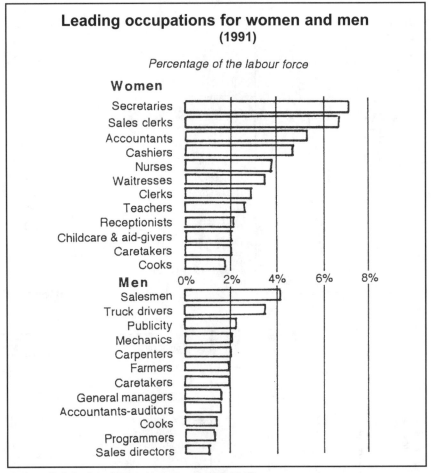

Leading occupations for women and men
(1991)

Percentage of the labour force

Women

Secretaries
Sales clerks
Accountants
Cashiers
Nurses
Waitresses
Clerks
Teachers
Receptionists
Childcare & aid-givers
Caretakers
Cooks

Men   0%   2%   4%   6%   8%

Salesmen
Truck drivers
Publicity
Mechanics
Carpenters
Farmers
Caretakers
General managers
Accountants-auditors
Cooks
Programmers
Sales directors

Source: Statistics Canada quoted in La Presse (1993 03 03)

Median net worth by occupation
(1998)

Occupation of main earner for family	% of family units	Median net worth ($)	Median after-tax income ($)
All family units	**100**	**81 000**	**33 400**
Management	8	192 800	56 100
Primary industry	2	155 900	35 800
Social science, education, government	5	112 200	49 600
Health	4	111 600	46 000
Natural and applied sciences	6	90 500	47 600
Trades, transportation and equipment operators	12	79 000	41 800
Business, finance and administration	10	77 900	39 700
No occupation	32	76 500	20 700
Processing, manufacturing, utilities	6	66 000	41 700
Art, culture, recreation. sport	2	65 000	35 400
Sales and service	13	40 000	28 400

*"**Net worth**" includes financial assets such as investments, property, and shares in funds and businesses.*
*"**Median**" is the point at which half the group fall below the median number and half are above it.*

Source: Statistics Canada

How interest rates affect mortgage payments

The figures are the monthly payments (principal and interest) for each $1000 of mortgage.
Example: *The cost per month for a $80 000 mortgage amortized over 20 years at 10% interest would be $9.52 x 80 = $761.60.*

Interest rate	Amortization period					
%	1 year	5 years	10 years	15 years	20 years	25 years
4.00	$85.13	$18.40	$10.11	$7.38	$6.04	$5.26
5.00	85.58	18.85	10.58	7.88	6.57	5.82
6.00	86.03	19.30	11.07	8.40	7.12	6.40
7.00	86.48	19.75	11.56	8.93	7.69	7.00
8.00	86.93	20.21	12.06	9.48	8.28	7.63
9.00	87.38	20.68	12.58	10.05	8.89	8.28
10.00	87.82	21.15	13.10	10.62	9.52	8.94
11.00	88.27	21.62	13.64	11.21	10.16	9.63
12.00	88.71	22.10	14.18	11.82	10.81	10.32
13.00	89.16	22.58	14.73	12.43	11.48	11.02
14.00	89.60	23.07	15.29	13.06	12.15	11.74
15.00	90.05	23.56	15.86	13.69	12.84	12.46

Source: The Royal Bank of Canada

Mortgage rates by year

Figures are percentages.

	1-year	3-year	5-year
1981	18.12	18.33	18.38
1982	16.85	17.83	18.04
1983	10.98	12.52	13.23
1984	12.00	13.21	13.58
1985	10.31	11.54	12.12
1986	10.15	10.88	11.21
1987	9.85	10.69	11.17
1988	10.83	11.42	11.65
1989	12.85	12.17	12.06
1990	13.40	13.35	13.35
1991	10.22	10.90	11.13
1992	7.87	8.95	9.51
1993	6.91	8.10	8.78
1994	7.74	8.99	9.42
1995	8.44	8.82	9.19
1996	6.25	7.37	7.95
1997	5.54		7.07
1998	6.50		6.93
1999	6.80		7.56
2000	7.85		8.35
2001	6.14		7.40
2002	4.70		7.01

Source: Canada Mortgage and Housing Corporation

Average resale value of homes

Amounts are in Canadian dollars.

CITY	1980	1990	2003
Canada	**67 044**	**143 379**	**208 525**
St. John's, Nfld.	53 246	88 939	124 468
Halifax, NS	53 160	97 238	158 634
Saint John, NB	45 170	78 041	106 674
Montréal, QC	49 419	111 956	173 813
Ottawa, Ont	63 177	141 562	225 381
Toronto, Ont	75 620	254 890	297 175
Regina, Sask	48 628	71 054	99 318
Calgary, Alta	93 977	128 484	212 342
Edmonton, Alta	84 622	101 040	167 846
Vancouver, BC	100 065	226 385	345 175
Victoria, BC	85 066	160 743	337 638

Source: The Canadian Real Estate Association

Consumer Price Index
(1915-2003)

1992 = 100

The CPI is the weighted average of a package of goods and services normally purchased by Canadian households.

1915	7.3
1920	13.5
1925	10.9
1930	10.9
1935	8.7
1940	9.5
1945	10.9
1950	14.9
1955	16.8
1960	18.5
1965	20.0
1970	24.2
1975	34.5
1980	52.4
1985	75.0
1986	78.1
1987	81.5
1988	84.8
1989	89.0
1990	93.3
1991	98.5
1992	100.0
1993	101.8
1994	102.0
1995	104.2
1996	105.9
1997	107.6
1998	108.6
1999	110.5
2000	113.5
2001	116.4
2002	119.0
2003	122.1
2004	
2005	
2006	
2007	
2008	

Source: Statistics Canada

The changing value of the dollar

The figures show how many current (2003) dollars would equal the purchasing power of one dollar in a specific year.

1915	$15.14
1920	9.04
1925	11.20
1930	11.20
1935	14.03
1940	12.85
1945	11.20
1950	8.19
1955	7.27
1960	6.60
1965	6.11
1970	5.05
1975	3.54
1980	2.34
1985	1.63
1986	1.57
1987	1.50
1988	1.44
1989	1.37
1990	1.31
1991	1.23
1992	1.22
1993	1.20
1994	1.20
1995	1.17
1996	1.15
1997	1.13
1998	1.12
1999	1.10
2000	1.07
2001	1.04
2002	1.03
2003	1.00

Source: Statistics Canada

Canadian inflation rate
(1915-2003)

The figures give the percentage increase in the Consumer Price Index from one year to the next. They are an indication of price increases.

1915	1.4
1920	16.4
1925	1.9
1930	-0.7
1935	1.2
1940	3.3
1945	0.9
1950	2.8
1955	0.0
1960	1.1
1965	2.0
1970	3.4
1975	10.9
1980	10.1
1985	4.0
1986	4.1
1987	4.4
1988	4.0
1989	5.0
1990	4.8
1991	5.6
1992	1.5
1993	1.8
1994	0.2
1995	2.2
1996	1.6
1997	1.6
1998	0.9
1999	1.7
2000	2.7
2001	2.6
2002	1.3
2003	2.6

Source: Statistics Canada

Canada's top financial institutions (2003)

Figures are in millions of $CAN

INSTITUTION	REVENUE	ASSETS	OWNERS
Royal Bank of Canada (RBC)	24 829	403 033	Many shareholders
Bank of Nova Scotia (Scotiabank)	17 261	285 892	Many shareholders
Canadian Imperial Bank of Commerce (CIBC)	17 122	277 147	Many shareholders
Toronto-Dominion Bank (TD Bank)	15 626	273 532	Many shareholders
Bank of Montreal (BOM)	13 147	256 494	Many shareholders
Mouvement des caisses Desjardins	7 712	94 652	Members
National Bank of Canada	4 665	82 423	Many shareholders
Caisse de dépôt et placement du Québec	3 662	118 838	Government of Quebec
ING Canada Inc	3 015	7 596	ING Netherlands
HSBC Bank Canada	1 997	37 509	HSBC Holdings, U.K.

Source: Financial Post June 2004

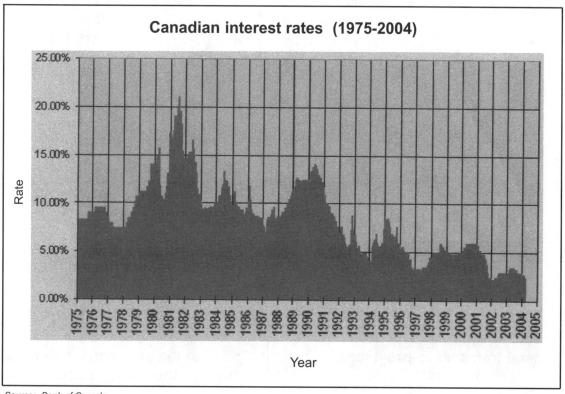

Canadian interest rates (1975-2004)

Source: Bank of Canada

Canadian income tax paid according to levels of income (1999)

Taxable income (in dollars)	Number of tax returns	As a %	Income tax paid ($ millions)	As a %
Under 10 000	5 296 830	25.01	114 801	0.14
10 000 to 20 000	5 049 460	23.84	2 860 238	3.56
20 000 to 30 000	3 334 830	15.74	7 015 240	8.73
30 000 to 40 000	2 591 130	12.23	9 839 539	12.25
40 000 to 50 000	1 751 710	8.27	10 316 967	12.84
50 000 to 70 000	1 866 380	8.81	16 578 593	20.63
70 000 to 100 000	800 390	3.78	11 257 936	14.01
100 000 to 250 000	409 720	1.93	11 426 890	14.22
Over 250 000	81 280	0.38	10 935 072	13.61

Source: La Presse (2002 09 26)

Who paid income tax in Quebec?

(2001 taxation year)

Tax bracket (total income)	Total returns %	% of total income tax paid
$0 to $15 000	39.1%	0.6%
$15 000 to $50 000	47.2%	39.4%
$50 000 to $100 000	11.7%	37.5%
$100 000 or more	2.0%	22.5%

Source: Canadian Taxpayers Association

Federal government spending (Selected departments)

Figures are in millions of dollars.

Department	1977-78	1987-88	1997-98	2001-2002
Agriculture	959	3 387	1 912	2 936
Environment	547	785	558	854
External Affairs	1 126	3 173	3 364	4 074
Finance	9 299	35 974	64 440	69 911
Fisheries & Oceans	-	609	1 152	1 512
Governor General	3	8	11	18
Human Resources	-	-	24 944	27 873
Indian Affairs	1 170	2 824	4 556	5 145
Justice	101	568	828	1 373
National Defence	3 771	10 850	10 187	12 254
Parliament	89	225	297	394
Public Works	808	2 925	3 757	4 442
Solicitor General	807	1 905	2 738	3 583
Transport	1 471	4 758	2 256	1 220
Veterans Affairs	841	1 612	1 935	2 247
TOTAL	**42 882**	**115 111**	**141 299**	**156 928**

Source: PublicAccounts of Canada

Federal government Annual surplus or deficit

Figures are in millions of dollars.

Year	Surplus or deficit	% of GDP
1960	-600	1.7
1965	-315	0.6
1970	+332	0.4
1975	-2 009	1.3
1980	-11 501	4.2
1985	-38 324	7.9
1990	-28 996	4.4
1991	-30 618	4.7
1992	-34 643	5.1
1993	-41 021	5.8
1994	-42 012	5.6
1995	-37 462	4.8
1996	-28 617	3.6
1997	-8 987	1.0
1998	+3 478	0.4
1999	+2 884	0.3
2000	+12 298	1.2
2001	+17 148	1.7
2002	+8 907	0.8

Source: Finance Canada

Federal transfers to provinces (2000-2001)

Province	Federal transfers $ millions	Budgeted expenditures $ millions	% of transfers
Newfoundland	1 475	3 709	39.8
Prince Edward Is.	341	883	38.6
New Brunswick	1 744	4 690	37.2
Nova Scotia	1 810	5 045	35.9
Manitoba	1 972	6 398	30.1
Quebec	7 309	48 253	15.1
Saskatchewan	941	6 373	14.8
British Columbia	2 715	22 300	12.2
Ontario	6 027	61 060	9.9
Alberta	1 444	17 709	8.2

Source: La Presse (2001 08 21)

How making loans increases the money supply

The figures are in dollars.

Stage	Chequing account deposits	Total of primary and secondary reserves (15%)	Excess cash available for loans
1	100.00	15.00	85.00
2	85.00	12.75	72.25
3	72.25	10.84	61.41
4	61.41	9.21	52.20
Total of all other stages	348.00	52.20	295.80
TOTALS	**666.67**	**100.00**	**566.67**

Canada's public debt

Net debt is the difference between what the government owes and what it is owed.

Net debt and interest figures are in millions of dollars. Per capita net debt and interest are in dollars.

	Net debt	Interest on debt	Net debt per capita	Interest per capita
1940	3 271	139	288	12
1945	11 298	409	936	34
1950	11 645	440	849	32
1955	11 263	478	718	30
1960	12 089	736	677	41
1965	15 504	1 012	789	52
1970	16 943	1 676	796	79
1975	19 276	3 164	849	139
1980	72 159	8 494	2 853	353
1985	199 092	22 445	7 911	892
1990	357 811	38 820	13 484	1 472
1991	388 429	42 537	14 424	1 590
1992	423 072	41 020	15 469	1 499
1993	466 198	38 825	16 301	1 356
1994	508 210	37 982	17 381	1 299
1995	545 289	42 046	18 435	1 420
1996	574 289	46 905	19 908	1 626
1997	583 186	44 973	19 247	1 484
1998	579 708	44 973	19 247	1 484
1999	576 824	40 931	19 166	1 353
2000	564 526	41 647	18 358	1 354
2001	547 378	42 094	18 242	1 403
2002	583 432	37 735	18 492	1 196
2003				
2004				

Source: Public Accounts Canada

Quebec's public debt

Year	Debt $ billions	As a % of GDP
1971	2 478	10.9
1972	2 920	11.9
1973	3 309	12.0
1974	3 679	11.8
1975	4 007	11.1
1976	5 134	12.4
1977	6 389	13.2
1978	7 731	14.6
1979	9 240	15.7
1980	11 870	16.9
1981	14 857	20.1
1982	17 812	21.8
1983	20 974	25.5
1984	24 425	26.5
1985	27 945	27.8
1986	31 631	29.4
1987	34 950	29.8
1988	37 702	29.3
1989	39 658	28.2
1990	42 819	29.3
1991	45 864	29.8
1992	51 249	32.9
1993	58 859	37.1
1994	65 643	40.3
1995	74 465	43.4
1996	76 510	42.6
1997	78 086	43.0
1998	97 732	51.7
1999	99 572	50.7
2000	100 546	48.3
2001	102 741	46.5
2002	104 850	45.0

Source: Ministry of Finance

Canada - US trade (1998 - 2003)

Figures are in billions of Canadian dollars

	Exports	Imports	Surplus	Value of $CAN
1998	269.3	233.8	35.5	67.43¢
1999	309.1	249.5	59.6	67.30¢
2000	359.0	266.5	92.5	67.33¢
2001	352.1	255.0	97.1	64.58¢
2002	347.0	254.9	92.1	63.68¢
2003	331.1	239.2	91.9	71.35¢

Source: Bank of Canada in La Presse (2004 02 17)

Canada - International trade in goods

Millions of dollars, balance of payments basis

	2000	2001	2002
Exports	425 587	414 638	410 686
Imports	363 432	350 623	356 109
Balance	**62 155**	**64 015**	**54 577**

Source: Statistics Canada

Canada - merchandise trade balance

Source: Statistics Canada

Canada - major trading partners
(2002)

Exports of goods	$ millions	%
United States	346 991	83.8
Japan	10 292	2.5
European Union	22 736	5.5
Other OECD	12 342	3.0
Other countries	21 945	5.3
All countries	**414 305**	**100.0**

Imports of goods	$ millions	%
United States	254 929	71.5
Japan	11 732	3.3
European Union	36 176	10.1
Other OECD	19 670	5.5
Other countries	33 952	9.5
All countries	**356 459**	**100.0**

Source: Statistics Canada

Leading world traders
(2003)

Exporters	Value $ billions	Share %
European Union	939.8	19.0
United States	693.9	14.0
Japan	416.7	8.4
China	325.6	6.6
Canada	252.4	5.1
South Korea	162.5	3.3

Importers	Value $ billions	Share %
United States	1 202.4	23.2
European Union	933.1	18.0
Japan	337.2	6.5
China	295.2	5.7
Canada	227.5	4.4
Mexico	173.1	3.3

Source: World Trade Organization

Canada - International travel balances

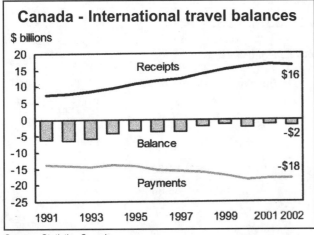

Source: Statistics Canada

Canada - Current account balances

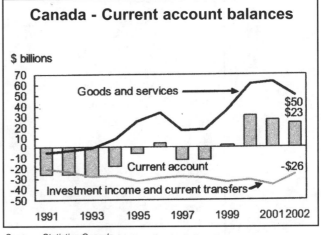

Source: Statistics Canada

Foreign currency exchange rates

Figures are annual averages given in Canadian dollars per unit.

	US dollar	British pound	French franc	German mark	Japanese yen	Euro
1998	1.484	2.459	0.252	0.845	0.0114	—
1999	1.486	2.404	0.242	0.811	0.0131	1.585
2000	1.485	2.250	0.209	0.701	0.0138	1.370
2001	1.549	2.231	0.211	0.709	0.0128	1.387
2002	1.570	2.358	—	—	0.0126	1.483

Source: Bank of Canada

Foreign aid
Largest donors

Figures are in millions of US dollars

1	Japan	13 508
2	United States	9 955
3	Germany	5 030
4	United Kingdom	4 501
5	France	4 105
6	Netherlands	3 135
7	Sweden	1 799
8	Canada	1 744
9	Denmark	1 664
10	Italy	1 376
11	Norway	1 264
12	Spain	1 195
13	Australia	987
14	Switzerland	890
15	Belgium	820
16	Austria	423
17	Finland	371
18	Saudi Arabia	295
19	Portugal	271
20	Ireland	235
21	Greece	226
22	South Korea	212
23	Kuwait	165
24	United Arab Emirates	150

Source: The Economist World in Figures 2003

Foreign aid
Largest contributions
as a percentage of GDP

1	Denmark	1.04%
2	Netherlands	0.86%
3	Norway	0.85%
4	Sweden	0.79%
5	Luxembourg	0.68%
6	Kuwait	0.44%
7	Switzerland	0.37%
8	Belgium	0.35%
9	France	0.32%
	United Kingdom	0.32%
11	Finland	0.31%
12	Japan	0.29%
13	Germany	0.27%
14	Portugal	0.26%
15	Australia	0.25%
	Canada	0.25%
	Ireland	0.25%
18	New Zealand	0.23%
	United Arab Emirates	0.23%
20	Austria	0.22%
	Spain	0.22%
22	Saudi Arabia	0.21%
23	Greece	0.20%
24	Italy	0.13%

Source: The Economist World in Figures 2003

Representative countries for different types of economies

(Dollar figures are given in $US)

	Gross Domestic Product US$ billions	GDP per capita US$	Agriculture % of total	Services % of total	Inflation % (2001)	Exports US$ billions	Imports US$ billions	Birth rate per 1000	Life expectancy male/female	Doctors per 1000 pop	Computers per 100 pop
Countries with a developed economy / MEDCs / Rich countries / The "First World"											
Canada	923	29 400	3%	74%	2.6%	250	219	11.0	76/83	2.1	39.0
United States	10 082	36 300	3%	74%	1.6%	689	1 177	14.1	75/80	2.7	62.3
United Kingdom	1 520	25 300	2%	73%	1.8%	274	330	11.3	75/81	1.8	36.6
Germany	2 184	26 600	1%	63%	2.4%	613	494	9.0	75/81	3.5	33.6
France	1 540	25 700	1%	74%	1.6%	300	298	11.9	75/83	3.0	33.7
Italy	1 438	25 000	5%	62%	2.7%	242	233	8.9	76/83	5.9	19.5
Netherlands	434	26 900	3%	75%	4.5%	215	187	11.6	76/82	3.1	42.9
Japan	3 550	28 000	5%	64%	-0.7%	406	327	10.0	78/84	1.9	34.9
Australia	582	27 000	5%	74%	4.4%	64	70	12.7	77/83	2.5	51.7
Countries that had a command economy in the past / Former "Second World"											
Russia	1 270	8 800	12%	59%	21.5%	101	44	9.7	62/73	4.2	5.0
Poland	368	9 500	19%	49%	5.5%	39	53	10.3	70/78	2.3	8.5
Romania	153	6 800	42%	30%	34.5%	14	19	10.8	67/74	1.8	3.6
Slovenia	36	18 000	11%	51%	9.4%	9	11	9.3	71/79	2.3	27.6
Countries with a growing industrialized economy / LEDCs / Sometimes called "Third World"											
China	6 000	4 600	65%	13%	0.7%	310	284	15.6	70/74	1.7	1.9
India	2 660	2 540	60%	22%	3.7%	48	54	23.8	63/64	0.4	0.6
Taiwan	386	17 200	8%	55%	0.0%	122	111	14.2	74/80	0.4	22.3
Brazil	1 340	7 400	23%	57%	6.8%	58	48	18.1	59/68	1.3	6.3
Mexico	920	9 000	21%	54%	6.3%	159	165	22.4	69/75	1.7	6.7
South Africa	412	9 400	30%	52%	3.4%	26	27	20.6	45/46	0.6	6.7
Saudi Arabia	241	10 000	5%	69%	-0.4%	68	31	37.3	67/70	1.7	6.3
Less-developed countries with a largely traditional economy / Sometimes called "Fourth World"											
Bangladesh	203	1 570	63%	27%	4.0%	5	8	25.1	61/61	0.2	0.2
Kenya	31	1 000	19%	61%	0.8%	2	4	27.6	46/48	0.1	0.6
Mali	9	840	80%	15%	5.2%	0.7	0.7	48.4	46/48		
Zimbabwe	28	2 450	26%	46%	74.5%	2	3	24.6	38/35	0.1	1.2
Haiti	12	1 700	70%	25%	14.2%	0.3	1	31.4	48/51		
Peru	132	4 800	45%	40%	2.0%	7	9	23.4	68/73	0.9	4.8
Somalia	4	550	71%	20%	100+%	0.04	0.05	46.8	44/49		

Sources: Canadian Global Almanac 2004 & The Economist World in Figures 2003